W9-CHC-885

Detection & Its Designs

Detection & Its Designs

NARRATIVE & POWER IN 19TH-CENTURY DETECTIVE FICTION

Peter Thoms

OHIO UNIVERSITY PRESS
ATHENS

Ohio University Press, Athens
1998 Ohio University Press, Athens, Ohio 45701

Printed in the United States of America

Ohio University Press books are printed on acid-free paper ⊗

05 04 03 02 01 00 99 98 5 4 3 2 1

Library of Congress Cataloging-in-Publication Data
Thoms, Peter.
Detection and its designs : narrative and power in nineteenth-century detective fiction / Peter Thoms.
p. cm.
Includes bibliographical references and index.
ISBN 0-8214-1223-X (cloth : alk. paper)
1. Detective and mystery stories, English—History and criticism. 2. English fiction—19th century—History and criticism. 3. Poe, Edgar Allan, 1809–1849—Fictional works. 4. Narration (Rhetoric) I. Title.
PR868.D4T48 1998
823'.08720908—dc21 97-35273

For Lisa

Contents

Acknowledgments

I have benefited from the assistance of many people during the past several years. For kind help and encouragement in a variety of professional matters, thank you to Kristin Brady, Paul Gaudet, Catherine Harland, Cameron McFarlane, Kerry McSweeney, and John R. Reed. Thank you also to the staff of Ohio University Press, particularly Nancy Basmajian, Holly Panich, and David Sanders. Most of all thank you to Lisa Zeitz for supporting this project in so many generous ways.

I gratefully acknowledge the financial assistance provided by a Social Sciences and Humanities Research Council of Canada postdoctoral fellowship and a Government of Ontario John Charles Polanyi Prize. A version of chapter 3, entitled "'The Narrow Track of Blood': Detection and Storytelling in *Bleak House,*" was published by the University of California Press in *Nineteenth-Century Literature* 50 (September 1995): 147–67.

Detection & Its Designs

Introduction

THIS STUDY ARGUES that nineteenth-century detective fiction is an inherently self-reflexive form, which exposes simultaneously the constructedness of its narratives and the motives underlying their creation. For the inventors and earliest practitioners of detective fiction, narrative is not what *is*—an unproblematic mirroring of events—but what *is made*, and that process of construction becomes the very subject of these works. In this context, the detective functions as an authorial figure, attempting to uncover the story of the crime,[1] and the "case" becomes a story about making a story. Thus the resulting solution confronts us as an artifice, as an intelligible chain of narrative constructed from discovered information and, significantly, from other documents. Indeed, in the number and variety of texts that the fiction contains —letters, newspaper excerpts, autobiographies, diary entries, reports, advertisements, handbills—we glimpse the very bricks of its structure, the linguistic pieces from which narrative and our apprehension of the *real* are assembled.

As my title suggests, the *designs* of detection are not only the neat patterns that investigation constructs, but also the motivations that guide these authorial projects. While the hunt for the criminal and his motives obviously provides a compelling structure for the new form, these early detective fictions become most interesting in the way that they turn back upon themselves to inspect the very motives that inspire the detectives and thus their findings. The detective's figurative writing emerges, I argue, out of a desire to exert control over others and sometimes (as in the fiction of Dickens and Collins in which detection becomes everyone's habit) over himself. In gratifying a desire to control others, detection often appears as an expression of egoism; here the writing or assembling of the case becomes a method of imposing power upon individuals, who are given characters and assigned places within the plot that the detective devises. Although the detective often emerges as an heroic figure whose efforts to transform mystery into meaning elicit the reader's identification and admiration, his[2] desire for authorial mastery disturbingly resembles the oppressive deeds of the criminal. Just as the criminal subjects his victims to his control, so the detective threatens the autonomy of individuals as he invades their privacy and attempts to define their identities. The detective often acts as if he were merely playing a game, a common image for his procedures, and one which suggests their potentially dangerous reductiveness. He simplifies the ambiguous and complex; he reduces characters to game pieces to be manipulated on a playing board; he proceeds on the premise that mystery represents a puzzle to be solved and a victory to be won. Indeed, the thrill of competition pervades the investigation, with the detective taking on not only the puzzle but also its author (the criminal) and, of course, any rival detectives who would presume to solve the mystery. Thus detection serves the detective's egoistic need to display his power, which derives from his storytelling skill. As a storyteller he defines his superiority, conquering the ostensible criminal by absorbing him and his deviant plot within his own controlling story, defeating his rivals by presenting a convincing narrative of explanation, and even, at times, disempowering his fellow characters and figurative readers by subjecting them to artfully contrived moments of shock and sensational revelation.

Early detective fiction, then, not only reflects authorial exuberance in intricate plotting but also reveals an extensive critique of narrative patterns and the compulsions that generate them. Within some of the finest stories of an age of great storytelling, we find this distrust of narrative, of its power and its effects on the social body. As these fictions suggest, narrative extends its negative influence not only upon those who, for example, are the unfortunate subjects of its reductive and oppressive stories, but also upon the tellers themselves. For often the imagery surrounding detection and storytelling characterizes that linked activity as a physically and morally debilitating perversion or disease—as an uncontrolled hunger for the hidden and private, a cannibalistic consumption of others' identities. Like cannibalism, which inevitably implies self-eating, detection rebounds upon its practitioners, both as a moral infection and, ironically, as a system of surveillance they have helped create. In Godwin's *Caleb Williams* the protagonist's initial act of detection sets in motion a series of intrusive deeds, transforming his world into a place of suspicion, defensiveness, and strife. The incessant watchfulness depicted in Godwin's novel also distinguishes *Bleak House* and *The Moonstone,* in which characters shrink from the scrutiny of all kinds of investigators: professional and amateur detectives, journalists, busybodies. Indeed, in this shrinking from real or, significantly, imagined detection we see how characters attempt to protect or regulate themselves.[3] While detectives often seek to control others, in this second type of detection they impose control upon themselves. Internalizing detection, they bring upon themselves a mode of self-control and repression that conceals the secretive or criminal side of the self.

My investigation of detectives, their storytelling, and their varying motives of control and self-control is rooted in discussions of works by five authors. Although the first detective story in English is generally considered to be Poe's "The Murders in the Rue Morgue" (1841), I begin a half century earlier with William Godwin's *Caleb Williams* (1794), one of the genre's most important forerunners. If not precisely a detective novel, it is nevertheless a novel about detection that, in depicting the trials of its amateur investigator, Caleb, delineates—perhaps more vividly than its successors—the relationships between detection, storytelling, and power. In *Caleb Williams* Godwin develops a myth about the dangers of detection and story-making, suggesting how those actions disrupt an original social harmony, drive individuals to turn against one another, and thus create the dreadful circumstances of "things as they are." The novel's startling secret, then, is not what Caleb's initial detection uncovers—that Falkland is a murderer—but rather what Caleb discovers only much later: the culpability of his own investigative storytelling. In other words, Caleb comes to detect his own detecting; the autobiography he writes as a narrative structure to vindicate himself and to imprison and thus condemn the character of Falkland eventually collapses as it increasingly becomes a self-conscious examination of its own telling. For storytelling, the novel suggests, is an egoistic demonstration of power, an act of self-performance in which the attempt to affirm a desired public identity depends upon the oppressive plotting of the stories (and thus lives) of others. What might initially seem to be merely a defense of self constitutes an offense to another, who responds by defending and then offending in turn, and so on until a society of competitive storytellers is rapidly formed. This is the divisive world in which Caleb's investigation and narration of Falkland's life assumes its place alongside the oppressive storytelling of both Falkland, who frames Caleb as a scoundrel, and Tyrrel, who tries to impose his vicious designs upon the lives of Emily Melvile and the Hawkinses. This is the world of Caleb's memoirs, a world which, according to the novel's logic, storytelling does not so much recount as create.

This notion that storytelling is not a harmless pastime practiced in isolation from the world but an activity implicated in shaping that world underpins my investigation in chapter 2 of Edgar Allan Poe's detective, C. Auguste Dupin. In the three stories that feature Dupin—"The Murders in the Rue Morgue" (1841), "The Mystery of Marie Rogêt" (1842–43), and "The Purloined Letter" (1844)—an opposition emerges between the otherworldly (the way detection is presented as an abstract, textual, game-like procedure) and the worldly (the way investigative writing is, in fact, entangled in the social reality of the here and now). Such a tension pervades Dupin's investigation of the murders in the Rue Morgue; his textual reconstruction of events seems to be at once in keeping and in conflict with his apparent devotion to seclusion and abstraction. Even as his undertaking is characterized as a private act—of reading newspaper reports, for example—the story conversely suggests how his detection operates transgressively as an overstepping of boundaries and an imposing of power. In "The Mystery of Marie Rogêt," this conflict reappears, as an apparently abstract and innocuous storytelling reveals its insidious side: its motives of securing money and honor, and its egoistic imagining and defining of character. The entanglement of narrative and power emerges most explicitly, however, in "The Purloined Letter," where the hidden text of detective fiction is given literal emphasis as a document of great importance, and where the investigator's authorial attempt to recover that text proceeds as a project of political consequence.

As part of its dual vision, Poe's fiction at least entertains the illusion of the detective as an intensely cerebral figure whose supposed isolation from the world allows him to mirror rather than create the *real*. In Dickens's *Bleak House* (1853), however, detection is so fully imbedded in the novel's world that it has become a habit, a way of being. The novel's interest is not limited to the investigation of a specific crime (Tulkinghorn's murder) by a specific investigator (the professional, Bucket), but rather broadens to encompass the widespread detection and storytelling of a society crippled by guilt. In *Bleak House* where the individual is burdened by a sense of innate depravity, detection arises both as an oppressive process of self-scrutiny in which characters police themselves and as a perhaps delusory attempt to escape such entrapment by investigating and thus writing others. As the former, detection is internalized so that the individual embodies a system of regulation, being both the oppressive law and its transgressor. At its most destructive, such self-regulation—the attempt to hide or repress one's criminal self—leads to self-obliteration, as in the examples of Nemo and Lady Dedlock. But the common anxieties of guilt and the desire for concealment are managed more effectively in the act of detecting others. In searching for the guilty secrets that define others, characters psychologically disfigure themselves. The outlaw becomes an enforcer of the law; the one who is vulnerable to detection and controlling narratives assumes a powerful position as a teller of stories.

Like *Bleak House,* Wilkie Collins's *The Moonstone* (1868) depicts a society coping with an oppressive system of surveillance. Just as Dickens's characters attempt to elude detection by practicing a detection that seemingly affirms their legitimacy, so Collins's Franklin Blake seeks to escape investigation by conducting an investigation that advertises his respectable self. In response to newspaper reporters, scandalmongers, and the general public, all of whom threaten to define his identity, Blake's investigative storytelling proceeds as an act of self-presentation. He proclaims his innocence by displacing his guilt onto another. Indeed, such displacement, *The Moonstone* suggests, is at the heart of the narrative structure of detection, which transforms a problem of pervasive guilt into a general suspicion that then vanishes when the specific criminal is identified. In the slow construction of the story—which Collins's multiple narratives superbly dramatize—we find not a statement of truth but an evasion of it. Blake's editing and narration emerge from his desire to control his self-image, a motive that marks his story-making as a repressive act, a blinkered vision, an anxious journey to a solution that will end speculation and effectively conceal the guilt and doubleness of his character.

Each of the works considered in this study undermines the authority of the detective, skeptically questioning his motives and hence his ability to stand apart from the social mystery he professes to explicate. The detective becomes part of that shadowy world, a figure whose ambiguity is often emphasized by his resemblance to the criminal. Such is the case in Arthur Conan Doyle's *The Hound of the Baskervilles* (1902), a novel which registers its distrust of the detective by revealing how Sherlock Holmes and the criminal, Stapleton, seek power in essentially the same way: by shocking and unnerving their chosen audience. Stapleton triumphs over his victims by contriving scenes of such extreme horror that Charles and Selden are literally scared to death, while Henry's nerves are shattered. Holmes, of course, does not kill anyone, but he nevertheless exerts his control over others by skillfully fashioning moments of intense surprise. What the novel critiques in this comparison is narrative power: how the construction of plot enforces an unequal relationship between the authority of the knowing creator and the enforced submission of his victims, who are subjected to manipulation and varying amounts of nervous trial. Indeed, narrative's capacity to upset and subdue is emphasized by the way it functions to preserve and disseminate the trauma of the original hounding. The manuscript of the legend repeats the nerve-racking episode for the Baskerville descendants; Stapleton recreates the chase scene for his victims; and Holmes and even Watson restage the terror and suspense in their authorial work of recovering the hidden story of the crime. Consequently, the detective storytelling that eventually defeats the criminal's plot represents not the eradication of oppression but its reappearance in the form of Holmes's own mastery and power.

This study argues that far from being a naive form, a positing of simple answers to profound mysteries, early detective fiction self-consciously grapples with the issue of storytelling itself. To pursue these inward-turning fictions is to uncover the detective's motives of controlling the representation of both himself and others, a discovery which in turn significantly undermines the authority of his solutions. Unlike the detective storytelling they describe, the fictions of Godwin, Poe, Dickens, Collins, and Doyle do not endorse the recovery of order and the imposition of closure. Instead, they expose story as a construction, inviting a kind of reading that counters the interpretive work of the detective, undoes his assertions of power, and turns us back again to the mystery.[4]

☾

In a recent book with Mark Olshaker, the FBI's famous criminal profiler John Douglas explicitly links detection to storytelling. Searching his childhood for a foreshadowing of his future career, Douglas declares:

> The one pursuit in school for which I did show a flair was telling stories, and this might, in some way, have contributed to my becoming a crime investigator. Detectives and crime-scene analysts have to take a bunch of disparate and seemingly unrelated clues and

> make them into a coherent narrative, so storytelling ability is an important talent, particularly in homicide investigations, where the victim can't relate his or her own story.[5]

What professional detectives "have to" do is piece together "a coherent narrative," and that job accords them power: they are the ones *entitled* to explain what happened. But the investigator's authority inheres not only in his official status as a representative of the law but also in his "storytelling ability," that "flair" which, in the career path Douglas retrospectively constructs, allows him to become a detective. If the detective hopes to exert a lasting impression upon his audience and to install his own version of events as the accepted truth, he must possess the narrative knack of organizing the evidence in a persuasive way.

Of course, a detective's chances of convincing others also depend upon the esteem in which both he and his profession are held. Persuasive stories rely upon reputable storytellers, a dependence which partly explains why detective fiction (with its emphasis on the process of solution) does not arise until the nineteenth century, when the detective begins to emerge as a more trustworthy figure. Ian Ousby, in his fine study *Bloodhounds of Heaven,* explains how the detective "entered fiction not as a hero, but as, at worst, a villain and, at best, a suspect and ambiguous character."[6] That image of the disreputable detective, which reflects the inadequacy and corruption of law enforcement in the eighteenth century, is gradually transformed as the occupation of policing itself becomes more professional and more respectable, particularly after the Metropolitan Police Act of 1829. A thief-taker like Gines of *Caleb Williams* (1794), who actually "fluctuate[s] . . . between the two professions of a violator of the laws and a retainer to their administration,"[7] gives way to the more attractive Inspector Bucket of *Bleak House* (1853),[8] whose very respectability underpins his narrative power. Just as the bewildered Sir Leicester Dedlock places his trust in Bucket, so it seems does the reader, who depends upon this figurative storyteller to convert mystery into meaning. We rely upon the detective to lead us out of the fiction's labyrinthine byways and, like any storyteller worth his salt, to entertain us in doing so.

The detective becomes, then, a literary character of considerable power, whose oracular pronouncements are anxiously awaited by his fellow characters and the fiction's readers. Indeed, the effectiveness of the detective is intimately connected to the demand for his stories, which the fiction represents in its images of a public hungry for secrets. The detective wields not only literary power (in artfully unfolding his narrative to a rapt and often astonished public) but also social power (in explaining the community to its members). And it is at this moment, when his voice seems most influential, that the detective perhaps becomes most oppressive and most dangerous. Certainly, the very fiction that celebrates the detective and awards prominence to his solutions simultaneously registers discomfort with his authority.[9] Who is this investigator? What are his motives? What gives him the right to control others—not only defining their identities by the stories he tells but also regulating their behavior by the stories he might tell? In exploring these issues detective fiction subverts its ostensible narrative project, questioning the remedial nature of a design that purports to untangle the complex, isolate the criminal, and provide the comforts of solution.

So even as detective fiction develops the narrative formula for its popular success, it remains suspicious of its storytelling and also its figurative storytellers, who are by no means limited to the professional detective. Indeed, one of the striking features of the form is its penchant for the amateur—for Caleb, Dupin, Guppy, Blake, and so on, not forgetting, of course, the numerous busybodies on the fringes of these works who add their own contributions to the speculative stew. Although he is without official credentials, the amateur is not thereby diminished in the eyes of the reader: he gleans the new respect accorded the practice of detection as well as any markings of moral, class, or intellectual *superiority* that the author cares to bestow. Moreover, the amateur represents the idea —dear to the reader—that potentially anyone, given sufficient curiosity, could conduct an investigation. That the amateur is not literally the hand of the law seems of little consequence when he can, like Dupin, pass his explanation to the authorities or simply publicize the information himself. For, after all, it is the word that punishes: the story that the detective constructs works in the figurative courtroom of society to exclude the wrongdoer.

The world of nineteenth-century detective fiction is populated with these storytellers who can make or break reputations, and who by their very (or suspected) presence pressure individuals to monitor carefully their behavior. Even we, as readers of the evidence, are figuratively conscripted into this drama of judgment, where characters are examined and tried on the basis of stories told about, or by, them. In this swirl of storytelling energy, where characters attempt to shape how they are perceived by others, the developing genre exposes how its preoccupation with plotting necessarily extends to character. For the two are interconnected: to study a work's plotting is to study how it conceives of character not as a stable given but as a product of a storytelling environment in which constant detective judgments of innocent or guilty, respectable or unrespectable compel defensive acts of self-performance. To what extent is a *real* individual a pose, a reputation, a construction like a character in a fiction? Conversely, to what extent must the complexity of the individual elude definition by the constricting social and fictive stories that attempt to label characters as either good or bad? Those are the sort of questions that detective fiction self-consciously raises and that its investigators do not answer. Although the narrative impulse of detective fiction becomes the celebrated catalyst for solution, it also—as these texts indicate—becomes the engine of that insidious power that weaves itself throughout these fictional worlds and imprisons their inhabitants.

In considering power in this study, I examine both the control wielded by the detective-storyteller and the forces compelling his narrative acts. What I don't pursue, however, is how these narratives of detective fiction work *powerfully* in the culture at large by endorsing or promoting certain ideologies of gender, class, race, etc. Important work has been conducted in this area[10] and will, no doubt, continue to be conducted. I have chosen to focus, instead, on power as it operates within the fictional worlds of selected works. My focus, then, is on close reading, which I hope illustrates how these texts self-consciously undermine their own power by critiquing their figurative storytellers and thus challenging or complicating whatever ideological positions are implicit in the investigations' analyses and solutions. In early works of detection, the authority inhering in successful inquiries is subverted, and nowhere perhaps is that subversion more powerfully rendered than in *Caleb Williams*.

ONE

Telling Stories

Narrative and Power in *Caleb Williams*

James Thompson has observed that "like a police detective . . . Godwin's procedure in *Caleb Williams* [1794] is fundamentally etiological, explaining criminal activity and injustices by working backwards to social inequality."[1] While acknowledging the importance of Thompson's insightful comparison, I suggest that the procedure of searching backwards from evidence of crime—the distressing condition of society—to a determining cause uncovers another culprit: the story-making impulse itself. In describing Caleb as an insatiable reader, panting "for the unravelling of an adventure" (4),[2] and then as an equally breathless detective, seeking to determine the secrets of Falkland's past, the novel establishes its interest in the human and ultimately tyrannical hunger to uncover or construct stories. Caleb's authorial act of oppression, as he threatens to imprison Falkland within a speculative narrative, is echoed by the activities of Falkland and Tyrrel, whose concern for the repute of their personal stories drives them to narrative machinations that deny the autonomy of others. In *Caleb Williams* storytelling is the force of discord, fracturing social cohesion, pitting individual against individual, generating the plotting and intrigue that frame the bleak world of "things as they are."[3]

In repudiating his own act of self-writing in the novel's final pages, Caleb calls himself Falkland's "murderer" (325), a judgment which may seem excessively harsh. Yet such a personal assessment forces us, nevertheless, to consider the parallels that Caleb apparently detects between his own treatment of Falkland and the cruel authority manifested by Falkland and Tyrrel. Not unlike Tyrrel's brutal attempt to plot the life of Emily Melvile or Falkland's efforts to frame Caleb within a narrative of disrepute, Caleb's subjection of Falkland to his own detective inquiry and then to the story he imaginatively engineers is an exertion of power, a radical constraining of a complex identity. For Caleb, Falkland had become merely a function within the designs of a narrative that is first held as private understanding (the existence of which is known only to Falkland) and then, finally, conceived as a written document and a spoken testimony to be presented publicly by Caleb with the intention of "vindicating [his] character" (326).[4] At the end of his narrative Caleb seems to assume his share of authorial responsibility for "things as they are"; he seems to recognize that in narrating the story of his world he is indeed implicated in shaping that world, building into it the very assumptions and structures of dominance and vulnerability that polarize his society.

Caleb Williams begins his memoirs with the comment that his "life has for several years been a theatre of calamity" (3), and in the fourth paragraph he suggests the original cause of his suffering:

> The spring of action which, perhaps more than any other, characterised the whole train of my life, was curiosity. It was this that gave me my mechanical turn; I was desirous of tracing the variety of effects which might be produced from given causes. It was this that made me a sort of natural philosopher; I could not rest till I had acquainted myself with the solutions that had been invented for the phenomena of the universe. In fine, this produced in me an invincible attachment to books of narrative and romance. I panted for the unravelling of an adventure, with an anxiety, perhaps almost equal to that of the man whose future happiness or misery depended on its issue. I read, I devoured compositions of this sort. They took possession of my soul; and the effects they produced, were frequently discernible in my external appearance and my health. (4)

Curiosity is the "spring of action" in two senses, for it is both the activating force that "gave," "made," and "produced" his behavior and character, and the inquisitive energies of desire, restlessness, and anxiety that drive him forward, initiating the series of events forming "the whole train of [his] life." Indeed, curiosity emerges as the source of story: curiosity is located as the origin or the "spring of action" of Caleb's tale and, more generally, it seems to be the instigator of story-making itself, the craving for knowledge that exists *as* narrative form. For the knowledge Caleb seeks is rendered by the narrative structures that relate "effects" to "causes," transform mysteries to "solutions," and—as the momentary climax to such pleasurable patterning of meaning—unfold fictional adventures to their "issue."

In the course of the fourth paragraph, then, Caleb's curiosity becomes identified with his passionate activity as a reader, and the pursued knowledge becomes equated with the complete "unravelling" of the line of narrative. Just as he, as a natural philosopher, "could not rest till [he] had acquainted [himself] with the solutions that had been invented for the phenomena of the universe," so he, as a reader, could not abide mystery but "panted" in his pleasurable haste to cross the narrative space of suspenseful incompletion and reach the resolving moment of conclusion.[5] By emphasizing Caleb's "invincible attachment to books of narrative," Godwin begins to develop the now familiar analogy between the passionate investigation of the protagonist-detective and the reader's own hunger to uncover the secrets of narrative. This identification, in which, figuratively, the reader is drawn into the text to perform the same tasks and experience the same thrills as the detective, skillfully fulfills the writer's ambition of engaging the audience, of creating, in Godwin's words (in his 1832 "Preface" to *Fleetwood*), "a powerful hold on the reader" (337). But, at the same time, the example of Caleb is, paradoxically, constructed as one that the reader should not want to embrace.[6] Even at the beginning of the novel his readerly enthusiasm seems dangerously excessive, his panting and devouring suggesting an uncontrolled appetite.

The cause-effect narrative that the novel unfolds and the fourth paragraph encapsulates is that reading and writing and detection —interchangeable metaphors describing the piecing together of narrative pattern—have negative consequences. As Caleb informs us, "compositions of this sort . . . took possession of my soul; and the effects they produced, were frequently discernible in my external appearance and my health." Gabriel Betteredge, the faithful steward of the Verinder household in Wilkie Collins's *The Moonstone* (1868), in seeking to explain how his own better judgment is conquered by his growing interest (and involvement) in Sergeant Cuff's inquiries, coins the phrase "detective-fever"—which in linking detection to disease suggests his subjection to both abnormal stimulation and moral infection. Caleb's description of how reading takes "possession" of his soul and registers its "effects" on his body establishes a similar diagnosis, connecting the love of narrative to disease that threatens the individual's physical and, especially, moral being. Of course, when we first encounter the fourth paragraph, the description of the effects of Caleb's reading may appear to be only a celebration of the intensely imaginative experience of the young. But his reading quickly loses its aura of innocence when a half-page later Caleb's attention shifts from books to a reading of Falkland, who is figured as a text demanding interpretation: "every muscle and petty line of his countenance seemed to be in an inconceivable degree pregnant with meaning" (5). Indeed, in nurturing an avid appropriation of others' experience, his youthful reading of fiction informs his inquisitive adult behavior: such early reading conditions the desires that compel him to investigate, to trespass the boundaries of the private, and to assemble those structures of meaning that oppressively define the identities of others. Significantly, then, *Caleb Williams* portrays the moral and physical effects of this early reading, consequences which the unfolding narrative proceeds to chart at length as Caleb's health is gradually worn away by the events that his own curiosity initiates.

The novel's presentation of Caleb encourages us to read him not only as an individual character interacting with other individual characters but also as a representative character demonstrating the typically human desire to impose narrative form. The symbolic dimension of Caleb's experience—emphasized by the title of the first edition, *Things As They Are; or, The Adventures of Caleb Williams*—enables us to see that the effects of the narrative impulse on Caleb's health represent the insidious damages wrought by storytelling on the social body itself. Furthermore, the suggested universality of Caleb's storytelling is reinforced by the way the novel depicts that act as a myth of original sin,[7] as the cause that alienates individuals from the possibility of social harmony and initiates them into a social world of power struggle and discord. Chronicling the path of his "ungoverned curiosity" (133), Caleb describes his determination to act as "a watch" and "a spy" upon his patron: "The instant I had chosen this employment for myself, I found a strange sort of pleasure in it. To do what is forbidden always has its charms, because we have an indistinct apprehension of something arbitrary and tyrannical in the prohibition" (107). Here his commitment to investigate and thus explain the mystery of Falkland suggests a stage in his fall as he sins against his "master" (107) in his pursuit of the "forbidden." Although Caleb's phrasing possibly betrays an attempt to justify the act, portraying it as an assertion of liberty against "arbitrary and tyrannical" constraints, the stressing of his "pleasure" and enjoyable "sensation" (108) frames his undertaking as self-gratification. He is not resisting unjust boundaries but expanding the territory of his dominion in an egoistic assertion of power.

This invasive act of storytelling, in which Caleb searches for the secrets that seem to define his patron's identity, climaxes with his pronouncement of Falkland's guilt. Studying Falkland's agitated behavior as he hears the evidence concerning "a man of benevolent character" accused of murdering "a human brute" (129), Caleb confirms his suspicions: " 'This is the murderer! the Hawkinses were innocent! I am sure of it! I will pledge my life for it! It is out! It is discovered! Guilty upon my soul!' " (129). What we have here is a trial within a trial[8] as the magistrate Falkland is judged by Caleb who adopts the law's terminology in reducing the mystery of character to the label "Guilty."[9] The very brevity and syntactical simplicity of these sentences imply Caleb's failure to comprehend Falkland and also his breathless excitement at this apparent moment of narrative resolution. He proceeds "with hasty steps along the most secret paths of the garden" (129), a description suggesting his physical agitation as he utters his verdict; his mental impetuousness as he reaches those conclusions (hastily tracing the full path and thus pattern of the narrative he possesses); and his transgression as he trespasses upon the "most secret" or forbidden part of the garden. Furthermore, in retreating into its most hidden regions to voice privately his judgment, he transforms the garden into a domain of deception and conflict, and thus experiences his fall.

In other words, Caleb has already opposed Falkland and the idea of community before Falkland discovers his disloyalty and exiles him. By exerting storytelling power Caleb causes the reaction of Falkland, who responds to this assault on his identity with the opposing force of his own aggressive and similarly invasive storytelling. By his own actions, Caleb thrusts himself into a vicious world of competing storytellers, where he experiences the division of his life into an "offensive part" (his investigatory plotting of Falkland's narrative) and a "defensive" (134) part (his reaction to the ensuing counterplotting). At the very moment when he seems to possess Falkland within the snares of his narrative, Caleb's own privacy and autonomy are assailed:

> In the midst of one of my paroxysms of exclamation, and when I thought myself most alone, the shadow of a man as avoiding me passed transiently by me at a small distance. Though I had scarcely caught a faint glimpse of his person, there was something in the occurrence that persuaded me it was Mr. Falkland. I shuddered at the possibility of his having overheard the words of my soliloquy. (130–31)

Whether the secrets of his soliloquy are overheard by Falkland is unclear; and perhaps that uncertainty is what makes Caleb potentially so vulnerable and the scene so unsettling. Such a reversal of power, as the detective is detected, anticipates that sensational moment in Collins's *The Woman in White* (1860) when Count Fosco reads of Marian Halcombe's investigations in her own diary. Of course, more immediately relevant is the scene one page later, when Caleb is discovered breaking into Falkland's trunk and is "overcome . . . by the horror of the detection" (132). Only then and only in reference to his own comfort does Caleb begin to sense the cruelty of detection as he, in his own dark and private moment, is subjected to scrutiny, to the potentially false interpretations of conjecture, and to the possibly violent storytelling powers of a man desperate to preserve his own reputation.

Caleb is unwilling to acknowledge his "fault" in precipitating his own calamity, arguing that the crisis in his affairs "proceeded from none of those errors which are justly held up to the aversion of mankind; my object had been neither wealth, nor the means of indulgence, nor the usurpation of power. . . . My offence had merely been a mistaken thirst of knowledge" (133). Yet as *Caleb Williams* suggests, the uncontrolled pursuit of knowledge (as embodied by narrative form) constitutes a sin, a "usurpation of power," and the novel underlines this point by representing the acquisition of another's secrets in terms of the more recognizable crime of theft. The assault on the trunk, which Caleb tries to excuse as an extraordinary action compelled by "mysterious fatality" (131) and "uncontrolable passion" (132), becomes an apt metaphor for his extended and calculated efforts to break through Falkland's mysterious shell to discover and possess the imagined explanatory truths of his inner being.[10] At one point in their conversation, exchanges manipulated by Caleb as part of his inquiry, Falkland accuses him of just such robbery: "Do you think I will be an instrument to be played on at your pleasure, till you have extorted all the treasures of my soul?" (118).[11] Only the victim comprehends the unjustness of the relationship, for Caleb himself seems blindly insensitive to the otherness of Falkland and to the cruelty of his own enterprise: callously, he uses Falkland as an "instrument" of his own "pleasure," plundering what seems to make that individual separate and unique merely to satisfy his own narrative hunger.

The supposed harmlessness of storytelling—Caleb is reluctant to admit wrongdoing and cites society's lack of "aversion" to the activity—is largely responsible for its insidious power. Without the normal constraints of the practitioner's conscience and fear of punishment and the victim's wariness, storytelling operates quite freely. It is this invisible power of narrative, its pervasiveness and allure, that constructs Caleb first as a reader and writer, and then as a victim and outcast as he experiences the oppressive weight of the false and widespread stories that express his identity. Although *Caleb Williams* considers despotism in its many guises, the structuring and imprisoning act of storytelling seems to be its most essential form, performing so easily and naturally the intrusive function of power Godwin describes in the 1794 "Preface":

> It is now known to philosophers that the spirit and character of the government intrudes itself into every rank of society. But this is a truth highly worthy to be communicated to persons whom books of philosophy and science are never likely to reach. Accordingly it was proposed in the invention of the following work, to comprehend, as far as the progressive nature of a single story would allow, a general review of the modes of domestic and unrecorded despotism, by which man becomes the destroyer of man. (1)

Indeed, fictional narratives intrude so effectively "into every rank of society" that Godwin employs an invented "story" as the appropriate vehicle to disseminate his message to "persons whom books of philosophy and science are never likely to reach."

If storytelling can be read as the unrecognized and thus "unrecorded despotism, by which man becomes the destroyer of man" (1), why does Godwin craft a fictional narrative and particularly one that is so compulsively readable? Part of the answer seems to be that, like *Don Quixote,* with which it shares an interest in questions of reputation, self-fashioning, and story-making, *Caleb Williams* critiques by example, employing the very narrative structure that it simultaneously rejects. While very different in tone from Cervantes's burlesque of romances, Godwin's novel undertakes its own examination of the human proclivity to impose pattern on experience by portraying Falkland's unfortunate attachment to the romantic paradigm and, especially, Caleb's various positions as reader, writer, and even character of narrative. Caleb's disenchantment from the thrall of narrative would seem to mirror the experience that the novel offers its readers, who become implicated in the narrator's investigations as he trespasses upon private space, who then witness the savage contention of storytellers that such a deed perpetuates, and who, finally, contemplate the significance of Caleb's denunciation of his actions in the novel's final pages. In depicting the figurative author's rebellion against the very narrative pattern he has been desperate to complete, the novel provides a needful counter-example to that full "unravelling of an adventure" (4) in which Caleb's (and possibly the reader's) sensibilities have been trained. While the seemingly benign reading material of Caleb's youth addicts him to the pleasurable movement to closure and to the mastery that the final position of understanding implies, his autobiography offers itself as an antidote to such craving, as a withdrawal from the model of power in which the author and the knowing reader come to possess the characters of their text.

The authority of the reader/writer and the subjugation of his object emerge in Caleb's description of his "incessant" observation of Falkland:

> There was indeed one eminent difference between his share in the transaction and mine. I had some consolation in the midst of my restlessness. Curiosity is a principle that carries its pleasures as well as its pains along with it. The mind is urged by a perpetual stimulus; it seems as if it were continually approaching to the end of its race; and, as the insatiable desire of satisfaction is its principle of conduct, so it promises itself in that satisfaction an unknown gratification, which seems as if it were capable of fully compensating any injuries that may be suffered in the career. But to Mr. Falkland there was no consolation. What he endured in the intercourse between us appeared to be gratuitous evil. (122–23)

While a comparison of this scene of reading with that found in the fourth paragraph of the novel emphasizes the visceral similarity of the two experiences, as Caleb in each thrills to the pursuit of "the end," such a juxtaposition also underlines a significant shift in Caleb's relationship to his reading material. In paragraph four Caleb appears to express an intense identification with the plight of the protagonist, panting "for the unravelling of an adventure, with an anxiety, perhaps almost equal to that of the man whose future happiness depended on its issue" (4). Although this sympathy for the other (which will help facilitate Caleb's eventual repudiation of storytelling) is present in his reading of Falkland, it has become seriously diluted by the urgency of his own "insatiable desire of satisfaction," a desire no longer compatible with the welfare of the read object. Consequently there exists a gulf, an opposition, an inequality, for the social "transaction" provides Caleb with the pleasures of observation and Falkland, by contrast, with "no consolation" at all, only the appearance of "gratuitous evil."

In the relationship of power formed out of this new textual situation, Caleb assumes both the pleasurable authorial function of explicating the mystery and the role of protagonist pitting himself against his antagonist Falkland, an enterprise whose risks supply the "tingling sensation, not altogether unallied to enjoyment" (107–8). Here, at the time of the initial investigation, Falkland is forced into an imagined textual design, his autonomy sacrificed to Caleb's emotional needs, just as later he is imprisoned as a character and subjected to the demands of Caleb's written account. Undoubtedly, Caleb creates the discord between himself and Falkland partly through a misguided desire for intimacy: he wants to bridge the gulf of social difference and mystery and know the other man. But even this motivation is self-serving and the consequence an act of trespass, as he intrudes where he does not belong. Yet as that favored character of novelists the orphan, Caleb desperately needs to belong, so much so that he conceives of Falkland, at times, as almost a heavenly parent, a figure whose virtues seem "almost too sublime for human nature" (107); later, as an outcast, he attempts to escape isolation by defining Laura Denison as his "mother" (298) and Collins as his "father" (315). What is common to these relationships is Caleb's authorial egoism as he imposes identities onto others. Indeed, in the novelistic world of *Caleb Williams* reading and storytelling are inherently egoistic and ultimately autobiographical. Even Caleb's supposed flight out of himself in identifying with the protagonists of his early reading seems somehow tainted and capable of being reconsidered as an inward flight in which another's experience is imaginatively refigured and felt as his own. He becomes the protagonist of these fictions, just as he becomes the protagonist, the daring adventurer "perpetually upon the brink of being countermined" (108), when he reads Falkland—or, perhaps more correctly, reads himself. For it is his own story that continually matters to Caleb as he passes from reading books, to reading Falkland, to that explicitly narrative act which finally becomes a highly self-conscious reading of himself.

☾

My purpose has been not to celebrate Caleb's many good traits, but to magnify his flaw, that egoistic impulse of storytelling responsible for corrupting Caleb and, by implication, the social body itself. For despite his goodness, Caleb is typical in his fall and in his subsequent entanglement in a web of plotting spun by himself and others. When Caleb applies the energy of his own reading and storytelling to Falkland, the squire responds by exerting his own narrative powers over Caleb, implicating him in a chain of events descending from the past and including most significantly the conflict of Falkland and Tyrrel. The oppressiveness of this anterior plot is acknowledged by Caleb in the writing of his own story, which first requires that he provide a history of Falkland:

> To the reader it may appear at first sight as if this detail of the preceding life of Mr. Falkland were foreign to my history. Alas, I know

> from bitter experience that it is otherwise. My heart bleeds at the recollection of his misfortunes as if they were my own. How can it fail to do so? To his story the whole fortune of my life was linked; because he was miserable, my happiness, my name, and my existence have been irretrievably blasted. (10)

Caleb's method and the work itself (with its complex interweaving of the stories and characters of Caleb, Falkland, Tyrrel, Emily, the Hawkinses, Gines, and others) portray a social world in which the individual life story does not unfold freely as a clean, self-directed line of action but is instead imbedded in, and thus constrained by, the rival plot-lines of others' stories. Yet even as Caleb acknowledges such dependency, his autobiography emerges as the psychological means of freeing himself from the trap of Falkland's narrative by rewriting that story and placing it within the context of his own.

After his release from prison in the third volume, Caleb is kidnapped by Gines and an accomplice and brought before Falkland, who offers him "one condition . . . upon which [he might] obtain some mitigation of [his] future calamity": "I insist then upon your signing a paper declaring in the most solemn manner that I am innocent of murder, and that the charge you alleged at the office in Bow Street is false, malicious and groundless" (282). This confrontation captures in miniature the conflict waged throughout much of the novel between the two willful combatants: Falkland, who wants to contain Caleb within the narrative he has devised, and Caleb, who refuses to submit to such a design. What is at stake, Caleb easily discerns, is his freedom to tell his own story and thus register his own identity; what "you require," Caleb tells Falkland, is that "I should sign away my own reputation for the better maintaining of yours" (283). Our sympathies, it would seem, are predisposed to embrace this champion of the individual's rights who bravely opposes the false plot authorized by Falkland and attempts to supplant it with the true story that has been repressed. Yet even as *Caleb Williams* engages its readers by precociously exploiting the conflict of innocence and truth with guilt and falsehood (a contest which would become central to the modern thriller), the novel refuses to endorse these dichotomies; it reminds us that just as Caleb is framed as a scoundrel, Falkland is also framed—forced into a narrative that will establish Caleb's reputation. Instead of being the solution to "things as they are," Caleb's storytelling promises only a continuation of the rivalry and an expansion of an increasingly complicated and oppressive textuality. Storytelling, as the conflict between Falkland and Tyrrel starkly emphasizes, is an expression of power; divested of its rhetoric, the rivalry between the two squires is reduced to a sudden brutal exchange. As Falkland's confession reveals, the murder of Tyrrel springs from his rabid protectiveness of his own "story," a self-identifying tale that has been snatched from him by the dishonoring blows leveled by his opponent. In knifing Tyrrel, Falkland reclaims his power over the "gigantic oppressor [who] rolled at [his] feet," but still he must continue to plot to secure his authority: "All are but links of one chain. A blow! A murder! My next business was to defend myself, to tell so well digested a lie, as that all mankind should believe it true" (135). Link upon link, the "chain" of this narrative lengthens, subduing Tyrrel, entrapping the Hawkinses, winding about Caleb, and even ensnaring Falkland himself, who is dragged down by the burden of his own deceit.

A significant commentary on the connections between storytelling, power, and identity is offered by Caleb's and Falkland's discussion of "how came Alexander of Macedon to be surnamed the Great" (110). Although provided by Caleb as an example of the conversations that sharpened his suspicions and inflamed Falkland's morbid sensitivity, the exchange illuminates both the individual's effort to construct identity and the potential fragility of that construction when assailed by public scrutiny. Defending the honor of Alexander and, it seems, himself from Caleb's implied criticism of the heroic ideal, Falkland exclaims,

> Did you ever read, Williams, of a man more gallant, generous and free? Was ever mortal so completely the reverse of every thing engrossing and selfish? He formed to himself a sublime image of excellence, and his only ambition was to realise it in his own story. (110)

Here Falkland argues for the success of Alexander's self-fashioning, portraying an unproblematic process of translating an initial "sublime image of excellence" into an enduring "story," which Caleb must surely have "read." Yet, as the novel illustrates, the autobiographical impulse—that prime mover of the novel's characters—often proves anything but glorious. Instead, the project of self-writing seems contaminated by the very egoism that inspires it; even Falkland's description of Alexander's undertaking communicates its self-centered and obsessive nature. The explicit charge of selfishness, however, is left to Caleb, who follows Falkland's "panegyric" with a damaging series of questions:

> But shall I forget what a vast expence was bestowed in erecting the monument of his fame? Was he not the common disturber of mankind? Did he not overrun nations that would never have heard of him, but for his devastations? How many hundred thousands of lives did he sacrifice in his career? (111)

Caleb's criticism indicates not only that such self-aggrandizing storytelling has an inevitable cost, but also that it will never achieve its desired success. The very fact of Caleb's criticism demonstrates that such stories exceed the control of their authors' intentions, becoming public property and thus subject to the varying interpretations of their readers. Falkland, however, in an attempt to preserve the sanctity of Alexander's text from the violence of Caleb's reading, offers the countercharge that Caleb's interpretation is itself an act of oppression: "You are not candid—Alexander —You must learn more clemency—Alexander, I say, does not deserve this rigour" (112). Of course by this point, as the agitation of the participants attests, the debate has achieved its real relevance as a commentary on the morality of both Falkland's self-writing and Caleb's interpretive re-writing of that story.

Not only do the characters of *Caleb Williams* attempt to establish and thus read their identities in the personal stories that they enact, but they also seem compelled to write those narratives on the public consciousness. The need to exhibit oneself publicly derives, in the examples of Alexander and Falkland, from a longing for fame; but even the least vain and ambitious seem to require some public confirmation of themselves. While Falkland desires to make his honorable character known to many, Caleb, in the misery of his isolation, recognizes the human need to be favorably known at least by a few:

> I endeavoured to sustain myself by the sense of my integrity, but the voice of no man upon earth echoed to the voice of my conscience. . . . To me the whole world was as unhearing as the tempest, and as cold as the torpedo. Sympathy, the magnetic virtue, the hidden essence of our life, was extinct. (308)

What Caleb craves is "sympathy," the self-confirming echo that will rescue him from solipsistic anxiety and acknowledge his place within a social world. Indeed, because the individual is a social animal, holding "necessarily, indispensibly, to his species" (303), he cannot avoid being known in some sense, however false; he emits signs which are then read by his immediate community. Moreover, the possibility of being misread or, worse, unfavorably read drives individuals to exert more and more conscious control over the public presentation of themselves. In the novelistic world of *Caleb Williams* identity is on trial, and the many hearings in which individuals are judged dramatize the processes of self-defense and inquisition permeating social relations. Advising Caleb on proper strategy at his own trial, Forester utters words that seem to describe that pervasive business of self-portrayal underlying the action and very writing of the novel:

> Make the best story you can for yourself; true, if truth, as I hope, will serve your purpose; but, if not, the most plausible and ingenious you can invent. That is what self-defence requires from every man where, as it always happens to a man upon his trial, he has the whole world against him, and has his own battle to fight against the world. (162–63)

Caleb Williams is preoccupied with the public and therefore textual nature of identity. As something that is both written and read, the public self emerges as a series of shifting and unreliable representations produced within the context of a constant trial. Against the specter of misreading that challenges their very ability to express themselves, individuals exert their storytelling power to "invent" and thus "make the best story" possible. Falkland, who perhaps best demonstrates how self-expression becomes performance, admits in the novel's conclusion, "I have spent a life of the basest cruelty to cover one act of momentary vice and to protect myself against the prejudices of my species" (324).[12] In one sense the decision to "cover" over his fallibility emerges as a method to "protect" himself "against the prejudices of [his] species" who, incapable of reading his character justly, would categorize him simply as guilty and a murderer. Yet his willful defense of his character results not only in the sacrifice of the autonomy of others, like Tyrrel and Caleb, but also in the paradoxical abnegation of his own freedom as he slavishly acts out the bold, clear strokes of a drama that accords with his audience's expectations. In forming, like his hero Alexander, "a sublime image of excellence" and attempting to "realise it in his own story" (110), Falkland initially seeks to allegorize himself and is apparently quite successful; Laura Denison, who "had been acquainted with the story of count Malvesi, and with a number of other transactions" (294), pronounces that Falkland's "name has been a denomination, as far back as my memory can reach, for the most exalted of mortals, the wisest and most generous of men" (300). But even though Falkland himself is eventually disillusioned by the act of murder that proves he is not a romantic stereotype, the social pressure to be the "image of excellence" continues. Entrapped by the romantic conventions he once idealistically endorsed, Falkland is reduced to wearing cynically the mask of honor and thus obtaining the favorable judgments of those like Laura who read allegorically and believe the "good man and the bad, are characters precisely opposite, not characters distinguished from each other by imperceptible shades" (299).

Tyrrel is also morbidly sensitive to how others perceive him, his insecurity magnifying and twisting others' displays of independence into elaborate counterplots that challenge his own authority. What exists externally and potentially as the threat of others' judgments is installed internally in the paranoid construction of an imaginative life where persecution and thus the need for one's own aggressive defense are ever present. To Tyrrel's mind even the "artless tale" (45) of Emily Melvile becomes rival storytelling that must be silenced and avenged. Initially Tyrrel manages to endure the "innocent eulogiums she pronounced of Mr. Falkland" (45), even when they begin to mount in intensity and frequency after her hero rescues her from a fire. "But the theme by amplification became nauseous, and he at length with some roughness put an end to the tale" (45). Although Tyrrel curbs her storytelling—which, in establishing "Mr. Falkland as the model of elegant manners and true wisdom" (45), implicitly undermines his own superiority—her silences become eloquent in celebrating his enemy:

> His imagination, ingenious in torment, suggested to him all the different openings in conversation in which she would have introduced the praise of Mr. Falkland, had she not been placed under this unnatural restraint. . . . Her partiality for the man who was the object of his unbounded abhorrence, appeared to him as the last persecution of a malicious destiny. He figured himself as about to be deserted by every creature in human form, all men under the

> influence of a fatal enchantment, approving only what was sophisticated and artificial, and holding the rude and genuine offspring of nature in mortal antipathy. (46)

This imagined scenario, in which even a family member deserts him for Falkland, registers Tyrrel's anxious fears of isolation and of the consequent depletion of his sense of self, which would no longer be mirrored in others. Tormented by his paranoia, he seeks to halt this perceived erosion of identity by brutally imprinting his power on others, thus ironically precipitating the social isolation he envisions. Tyrrel responds to Emily's storytelling by viciously exerting his own writerly control and attempting to confine her within a series of entrapping structures: the enclosure of her apartment, the plot involving rape and forced marriage to Grimes, and finally the jail where she is imprisoned "for a debt contracted for board and necessaries for the last fourteen years" (81). Similarly, when Hawkins dares to oppose his will, Tyrrel is driven to declare his proprietorship of this character, first in words—"I made you what you are; and, if I please, can make you more helpless and miserable than you were when I found you" (70)—and then in actions designed to manifest his authorial power.

Of course, wealth and social position confer authority and establish storytellers like Falkland and Tyrrel as formidable opponents. This social influence undergirds Tyrrel's deployment of the law against Emily and the Hawkinses, and leads Falkland to boast to Caleb of his "unsurmountable power": "prepare a tale however plausible, or however true, the whole world shall execrate you for an impostor" (154). Yet behind their bravado both characters are deeply insecure and vulnerable. Just as Falkland, pressured by scrutiny, defensively plays the role of the honorable man, so Tyrrel, sensing his own might and identity slipping away, desperately performs his acts of brutality to make his power visible to both others and himself. Tyrrel, however, is unwilling to acknowledge his status as a performer; indeed, in the midst of his torment as he imagines Falkland's increasing popularity and his own consequent isolation, he mounts a psychological defense by defining Falkland as "sophisticated and artificial" and himself as "the rude and genuine offspring of nature" (46). Often Tyrrel protects himself with such distinctions, arguing that those "that seem better than their neighbours are only more artful" (27), and wondering if all are "incapable of saying what kind of stuff a man is made of? caught with mere outside? choosing the flimsy before the substantial" (36). Surprisingly, Tyrrel proves prescient in charging Falkland with artfulness, but his argument falters when he himself resorts to the craft of rhetoric in portraying his own identity as "genuine," "substantial," and natural. Tyrrel is particularly irritated by Falkland's skillful use of words as a poet and conversationalist, but he fails to recognize his own indebtedness to language in his critiques of his opponent and in his exhibitions of physical strength that also rely on a sign system. After a meeting in which Falkland argues for a cessation of the quarrel between them, Tyrrel unburdens "the tumult of his thoughts to his confidential friend," attempting to defuse the power of Falkland's rhetoric by inquiring "what signifies prating?" and wondering that he "did not kick him! But that is all to come" (31). When the kicking does come as a response to Falkland's verbal denunciation in their final confrontation, the distinction between words and actions does not hold, for Tyrrel's violence clearly functions as artful self-expression, as a bullying show of authority. The opposition that Tyrrel tries to construct between the outer person of artifice and the inner person of substance collapses, unsettling the novel with questions about the nature of the self: whether it is merely a plausible fabrication, a disguise, or whether a more genuine identity might be located beneath or outside the clash of writerly performance and readerly misconstruction.

Does the Caleb who perseveres against Falkland and oppression, claiming "the more I am destitute of the esteem of mankind, the more careful I will be to preserve my own" (283), have an identity to protect? What is that identity? Where is it to be found? These are the questions the novel engages as it traces Caleb's responses to tyranny: the developing fortitude and flight from persecution, the decision to present his self-justifying story, and the confession that his narrative eventually becomes.

☾

Caleb, who graduates into this desperate world of storytelling through his own investigations of Falkland, now feels for himself the oppressive constraints that the watchfulness of others imposes. Caleb, whose own inquiry culminates in Falkland's confession, now suddenly becomes the object of a detection that in its constancy, scope, and intensity magnifies and thus makes explicit the coercion inhering in his own acts of surveillance.[13] Initially, as he remains in Falkland's employ, Caleb's freedom is curtailed not only by his master's effort to "prescribe" literally his "conduct" (143), but also by the pressure of scrutiny which regulates his behavior in an indirect but even more powerful way:

> I was his prisoner: and what a prisoner! All my actions observed; all my gestures marked. I could move neither to the right nor the left, but the eye of my keeper was upon me. He watched me and his vigilance was a sickness to my heart. (143)

While the passage explicitly portrays Caleb as the "prisoner" and Falkland as his "keeper," it implicitly suggests that Caleb becomes his own jailer—for the very effectiveness of the controlling "eye" depends on Caleb's awareness of it and thus of his internalization of its disciplinary function.[14] Such self-scrutiny instills a "sickness" of "heart," robbing him of the "freedom" of "thoughtlessness" (143) and fueling his desire to escape Falkland's presence. But when he flees, Falkland simply extends his power, falsely branding Caleb as a criminal and thus subjecting him to the suspicious gaze of not one man but society itself.

In framing Caleb, Falkland self-consciously employs the story as an imprisoning structure designed to control the individual. By constructing his employee as a scoundrel, Falkland severely undermines the authority of Caleb's own voice, initiates the chain of actions leading to his literal incarceration, and establishes the characterization that continues to haunt and govern him after his escape. Falkland's story is then disseminated by the handbills Forester supposedly authorizes, which provide "the description of a felon with the offer of a hundred guineas for his apprehension" (223); and that text is in turn supplemented by the longer narrative of "the halfpenny legend" (273) devised by Gines. Together these narratives attempt to trace Caleb in the senses of tracking the fugitive and returning him to custody, and of delineating who he is and thus invalidating his own effort of self-expression. Caleb loses control of his self-presentation and endures silently as he hears his "story bawled forth by hawkers and ballad-mongers" and his "praises as an active and enterprising villain celebrated among footmen and chambermaids" (274). " 'Here you have the most wonderful and surprising history, and miraculous adventures of Caleb Williams' " (268) cries a hawker, suggesting that Caleb's story and identity are contained in the halfpenny paper and hence exist now as possessions to be bought and sold and recirculated as gossip. When Caleb reads his published story, "despair" settles in his heart:

> The actual apprehension that I dreaded, would perhaps have been less horrible. It would have put an end to that lingering terror to which I was a prey. Disguise was no longer of use. A numerous class of individuals, through every department, almost every house of the metropolis, would be induced to look with a suspicious eye upon every stranger, especially every solitary stranger, that fell under their observation. The prize of one hundred guineas was held out to excite their avarice, and sharpen their penetration. It was no longer Bow-Street, it was a million of men, in arms against me. Neither had I the refuge, which few men have been so miserable as

> to want, of one single individual with whom to repose my alarms, and who might shelter me from the gaze of indiscriminate curiosity. (269–70)

The imagery of the hunt, of the ravenous search for the "prey" who has no "refuge," powerfully renders Caleb's vulnerability before a pursuing public that seems intent on consuming him. While Caleb's physical well-being is certainly endangered, the novel seems most interested in conveying the public threat to his psyche—how his own sense of identity is imperiled as his story passes into the mouths of a hungry public, and as he himself is forced to become an outlaw in avoiding detection. Fleeing from the greedy gaze of the public, Caleb goes into hiding, adopting the disguises that shut him away from society, friends, and even himself.

As Caleb acknowledges, "actual apprehension" seems perhaps preferable to his current condition, which adds the punishment of a "lingering terror" of detection to that highly effective state of imprisonment or exile that he himself enforces. In his fearful reaction to public scrutiny, which he eventually imagines as "a million of men, in arms against" him, Caleb turns inward, imposing a regimen of self-scrutiny and control:

> I shrunk from the vigilance of every human eye. . . . I was shut up a deserted, solitary wretch in the midst of my species. I dared not look for the consolations of friendship; but, instead of seeking to identify myself with the joys and sorrows of others, and exchanging the delicious gifts of confidence and sympathy, was compelled to centre my thoughts and my vigilance in myself. My life was all a lie. I had a counterfeit character to support. I had counterfeit manners to assume. My gait, my gestures, my accents were all of them to be studied. I was not free to indulge, no not one, honest sally of the soul. (255–56)

The process by which the external "vigilance of every human eye" compels the internal "vigilance in myself" anticipates those acts of self-supervision in *Bleak House* by which characters attempt to elude investigation. Indeed both novels portray a society under surveillance, where detectives create anxiety, and anxiety in turn invests detectives with supernatural powers, so that Dickens's Bucket and Tulkinghorn seem omnipresent, and Caleb questions whether Falkland's "power reach[es] through all space, and his eye penetrate[s] every concealment" (240). In their desire for concealment Lady Dedlock and Nemo of *Bleak House* pass beyond disguise to the complete effacement of themselves in death; but Caleb stops short of the suicide he contemplates (270). Yet for Caleb maintaining "a counterfeit character" seems to become a slow act of self-obliteration in which every "honest" impulse of the "soul" is suffocated beneath the need to give a "studied" performance and live a "lie." Recognizing his impending destruction, Caleb begins to reassert himself, doffing the physical disguises in which he had been immured and, most significantly, undertaking to tell his own story to the public.

Although Caleb wields power (however thoughtlessly and ineffectively) in his initial, private investigations, he later demonstrates integrity and a certain heroism in his reluctance to become a public opponent of Falkland's reputation. Only when he is betrayed by Spurrel and apprehended by Gines does Caleb go "before the magistrates . . . fully determined to publish those astonishing secrets, of which [he] had hitherto been the faithful depository" (275). After considerable suffering, through which he had remained loyal to Falkland, Caleb is driven toward public storytelling, which is simultaneously a defensive and offensive act—protecting and affirming the position of the author through its strategic and reductive treatment of other characters. Caleb attempts "to turn the tables upon [his] accuser" (275) and thus seat himself on the right side of the law, where instead of being the victim of suspicion and accusation, he may judge. Storytelling, the novel suggests, is grounded in a world of trial—of prosecution and defenses, charges and countercharges—and Caleb now clearly understands this legal context of narrative as here he (unsuccessfully) tries to charge Falkland with murder, and as he later begins his written account. For of his memoirs he writes, "I conceived that my story faithfully digested would carry in it an impression of truth that few men would be able to resist; or at worst that, by leaving it behind me when I should no longer continue to exist, posterity might be induced to do me justice" (303–4).

But Caleb also writes from "a desire to divert [his] mind from the deplorableness of [his] situation" (3), and initially this occupation provides a "melancholy satisfaction." "I was better pleased to retrace the particulars of calamities that had formerly afflicted me, than to look forward, as at other times I was too apt to do, to those by which I might hereafter be overtaken" (303). Writing, however, eventually and inevitably becomes "a burthen" (304). For only so long could his autobiography provide a therapeutic distraction from the anxieties of an unknown future and an artistic means to assert personal order over previous calamities. Gradually the gap between the writing present and the recollected past narrows until Caleb is once more faced with the prospect of current circumstances, over which he can exert little if any authorial direction. He can only record events as they happen to him, a position in which he is tortured by the frustration of passivity and the suspense of uncertainty. Anxious and fearing for his reason, Caleb conceives of a final offensive of storytelling as a means of gaining emotional relief—of forcing a conclusion and thus imposing a final form on events: "I desired to know the worst; to put an end to the hope, however faint, which had been so long my torment; and above all to exhaust and finish the catalogue of expedients that were at my disposition" (318). "I will unfold a tale—!" (314) Caleb writes, conveying his intention to act and, particularly, to assume narrative control in both denouncing Falkland and supplying closure to his memoirs. For challenging Falkland before the magistrate and completing his written project become coincident activities, a conjoining that illuminates the autobiographical emphasis of the accusation and the legal emphasis of the autobiography.

Thus the novel winds down toward a final confrontation between the arch-storyteller Falkland and the underdog Caleb, who arms himself for battle with both an oral and written narrative. "I will use no daggers!" (314) Caleb declares, realizing that he possesses a more violent and effective weapon in "this little pen" that will "stab [Falkland] in the very point he was most solicitous to defend!" (315). But at the very moment when he meets Falkland and his attack should begin, Caleb withdraws from the conflict, recognizing, he writes, that there "must have been some dreadful mistake in the train of argument that persuaded me to be the author of this hateful scene" (320). Indeed, what had been anticipated as a final showdown would have been only another clash in the continuing struggle for storytelling power, a pattern from which Caleb now escapes by exchanging a language of accusation and power for that of confession. The "shock" of seeing Falkland, who possesses "the appearance of a corpse" (318), awakens pity and compassion in Caleb, who no longer faces an opponent but a fellow-sufferer for whom he feels responsibility. From judging others Caleb turns inward to "the bar of [his] own conscience" (320), where he charges himself with "an overweening regard to [self] which has been the source of [his] errors" (325).

In his desire to "confess every sentiment of [his] heart" (320), Caleb abandons that legally informed storytelling in which the characters of others are judged and created in the act of self-defense. Caleb proclaims: "I came hither to curse, but I remain to bless. I came to accuse, but am compelled to applaud" (323). In repudiating his storytelling—in turning from accusation to a self-conscious examination of his own motives for telling—Caleb paradoxically redeems his story, transforming it from an aggressive and simplistic disclosure into a narrative that acknowledges both his own and Falkland's complexities. An awareness of Caleb's innocence is now supplemented by an awareness of his guilt, just as the portrayal of Falkland as a "murderer" (321) is balanced by his testimony that "Mr. Falkland is of a noble nature" (323). In his concluding words, Caleb underlines the shift in his narrative intentions:

> I began these memoirs with the idea of vindicating my character. I have now no character that I wish to vindicate: but I will finish them that thy story may be fully understood; and that, if those errors of thy life be known which thou so ardently desiredst to conceal, the world may at least not hear and repeat a half-told and mangled tale. (326)

A "half-told and mangled tale" is the story as it would have been: incomplete, biased, motivated by self-interest and the desire for power. But the addition of the confession revises and completes that story, making it, in Caleb's words, "a plain and unadulterated tale" (323). The honesty and comprehensiveness of his account is even admitted by Falkland, who praises Caleb for telling an "artless and manly story" that leaves him "completely detected" (324).

Falkland's comments remind us of Caleb's earliest investigations and suggest that only now has he achieved some success as a detective and storyteller in search of truth. He uncovers who Falkland is, but more importantly, and as the prerequisite for that discovery, he also detects himself. If storytelling is inherently autobiographical, then the most appropriate narratives attempt to thwart their own self-interested designs by becoming self-conscious acts of confession. As Caleb remarks, "I . . . believed that the conduct now most indispensibly incumbent on me, was to lay the emotions of my soul naked before my hearers" (320). This intention of uncovering the naked self echoes Godwin's description of his own "vein of delineation" in *Caleb Williams*, "where the thing in which my imagination revelled the most freely, was the analysis of the private and internal operations of the mind, employing my metaphysical dissecting knife in tracing and laying bare the involutions of motive" (339). Like Godwin, Caleb attempts to penetrate the stereotype, the performance, the disguise that convention and the pressure of public judgment enforce, and to uncover if not the true self at least a more complex and accurate portrait of the individual. Caleb now speaks as if from the source—his naked "heart" and "soul" (323)—delivering a truth that seems to stand in opposition to the earlier falsehoods of self-performance and misreading. What Caleb finally places his faith in is "the sovereignty of truth" (323) or the power of openness itself, which can supposedly disassemble the barriers that suspicion and the desire for power erect. The "frank and fervent expostulation . . . in which the whole soul was poured out," which Caleb wished he had given privately and which, he argues, Falkland "could not have resisted" (323), now touches Falkland who, in fact, "could no longer resist. He saw my sincerity; he was penetrated with my grief and compunction. He rose from his seat supported by the attendants, and . . . threw himself into my arms" (324). Just as Caleb's initial act of storytelling is figuratively the "spring of action" (4) that causes division and disorder, so his confession is suggestively poised as the trigger of a potential chain reaction that begins with Falkland's admissions. Although the novel's focus is on two characters, Caleb and Falkland, the breakdown and renewal of their relationship seems to offer a social myth of a fall (in which individuals are alienated by competitive storytelling) and of a possible partial redemption (in which the community might be reunited by the openness and sincerity of confessional acts). The world of the novel's end is still, of course, "things as they are," with Falkland dead and Caleb cast down in misery. But by its very structure, which moves to the confessions of Caleb and Falkland and their embrace—a scene in which the legal framework represented by the magistrate has all but vanished—the novel implies the idea of a better society that waits to be realized.[15]

Although the consequences of judging real people are far different from those attending discussions of fictional characters, the confessional fervor of the novel's close may inspire readers (like me) to acknowledge their own desire for power over the literary text. It perhaps goes without saying that a reading presents itself as only a meditation on a continually elusive work; but writing about a novel that is itself about the dangers of interpretation may easily instill doubts about one's own motives and agendas. The attraction of confessing at the end of one's argument is convenience: one has already allowed oneself the opportunity to wield power, and one may now assume the morally superior position of recognizing (or pretending to recognize) one's past folly. A similar taint of convenience haunts the ending of *Caleb Williams*, which seems to gratify every wish that Caleb might have harbored under the law while simultaneously sheltering this hero from charges of vindictiveness from both listeners and readers. Of course, maybe that is the point: Caleb triumphs by abandoning self-interest and not trying to triumph. But a novel about "things as they are" encourages not only hope in the transforming power of selfless sincerity, but also suspicion and cynical inquiry into possible motivations for actions.

Perhaps Caleb's concluding argument about "the sovereignty of truth" (323) is perched somewhat unsteadily on the idea of speaking directly from the naked heart or soul, a source of knowledge that is somehow free of the contaminants that pollute other acts of self-expression. Falkland describes confession as "the language of [the] heart" (136)—but the heart itself still remains hidden. Furthermore, one could argue that Caleb merely exchanges one pose (represented by his self-defensive narrative) for another (represented by the narrative of confession in which he accuses himself). "To confess," Tilottama Rajan has shrewdly remarked, "is to invent a cause to explain a series of effects that may elude such explanation."[16] Caleb's self-expression is still, it might seem, artificially organized in terms of narrative design, but now instead of imposing a structure that oppresses others he employs one that polices himself. The external system of law represented by the magistrate is all but invisible in the final trial not because it has been transcended but because it has been relocated: Caleb and Falkland have internalized its function and now inflict judgment upon themselves.

These objections complicate our response to the ending, but they do not invalidate the positive significance of Caleb's confession. While *Caleb Williams* still depicts the deployment of a system of control in self-regulation, such restraint seems necessary in a novelistic world plagued by egoistic storytelling. Judgment, it would seem, is effective only when it is self-administered. Moreover, in confessing Caleb does not imprison himself in a new structure so much as he manages to destabilize his narrative designs, attaining a textual complexity that seems liberating: the narrative of vindication is unsettled by his admission of guilt, just as the structure of confession is subverted by his accusation of Falkland. Although Caleb does not escape from the webs of language and narrative, his attempt to burrow more deeply into the complexities of who he is and to openly divulge that self seem nevertheless sufficient to exemplify the kind of discourse society needs. That is, of course, if Caleb is sincere. To entertain even the slightest doubt of Caleb's integrity is enough to fracture the condition of sympathetic inclusiveness that the confessions promote. Indeed, even as the novel envisions a possible means of social renewal, it seems to encourage its readers in the questioning skepticism that would frustrate such a project. Does the final glimpse of

Caleb present a character heroically suffering self-knowledge, or a character cynically (or practically) controlling his story so successfully that no one can tell it is a performance? After Caleb fails miserably to convince his audience of his innocence in his first trial, Forester advises: "Defend yourself as well as you can, but do not attack your master. It is your business to create in those that hear you a prepossession in your favour. . . . If you desire to be believed honest, you must in the first place show that you have a due sense of merit in others" (172–73). Has Caleb finally absorbed the worldly lesson that he should try to create sympathy in his audience? Does he betray pride in his craft when he details the tearful response of his listeners and particularly the reaction of Falkland, who even considers whether the confession is "a new expedient to gain credit" (324) before submitting to the emotional power of the tale? These are questions we might ask about real people—and even about a literary character like Caleb who, as a tantalizing collection of signs and clues,[17] allows us to re-experience both our desire for the truth and our recognition that it is always withheld.

TWO

The Stories of Poe's Dupin

Caleb Williams strips storytelling of its innocuous veneer to expose its sinister motives. In the novel's opening chapters Caleb's narrative appetite, like the reader's curiosity, seems relatively innocent and harmless: he indulges his private passion first in reading books and then—in a shift that might initially appear equally harmless—in reading his mysterious employer. But through Godwin's depiction of his latter act—of Caleb's reading, detecting, and writing of Falkland—we eventually discern that narration is an oppressive assertion of power and that the storymaking of Caleb, Falkland, and Tyrrel does not so much reflect as create "things as they are."

In turning now to Poe's amateur investigator, Monsieur C. Auguste Dupin, we again confront the issue of the detective's storytelling and how it situates him in relation to the shadowy world he attempts to describe. Certainly the three stories involving Dupin,

"The Murders in the Rue Morgue," "The Mystery of Marie Rogêt," and "The Purloined Letter," entertain the notion of the detective as a reclusive figure, whose very retirement from the world might seem to guarantee his objective vision of that world. Indeed, even more than Caleb, Dupin emerges as a bookish character, whose devotion to the imaginative life serves (as it does for Caleb) as a kind of proof of his disinterest when his investigations extend to *real* people. But as in *Caleb Williams,* the story of the investigation seems to curl self-consciously back on the investigator, pondering his pretense of innocence, his motives, and his own disposition to worldliness and power. In "The Murders in the Rue Morgue," Dupin's incursions into private spaces, such as the minds of the narrator and the sailor, are suggestively aligned with the more violent intrusions of the sailor, who invades the habitat of the orangutan, and of the orangutan, who breaks into the home of Madame and Mademoiselle L'Espanaye. Dupin's presumption of inhabiting the minds of other characters reappears in "The Mystery of Marie Rogêt," where the detective adopts the voices of both the dead victim and the character he posits as the criminal. Indeed, Dupin in these stories emerges as an egoistic storyteller who seeks to wield his power over both the characters he imaginatively defines and the rival detectives who might challenge his narrative authority. The issue of storytelling, however, is most powerfully examined in "The Purloined Letter," where the tale's plot involving the theft and recovery of a document of personal and political significance explicitly engages the relationship between narrative control and power.

"The Murders in the Rue Morgue"

In the sixth paragraph of "The Murders in the Rue Morgue" (1841), the narrator introduces the character of Dupin:

> Residing in Paris during the spring and part of the summer of 18—, I there became acquainted with a Monsieur C. Auguste Dupin. This young gentleman was of an excellent—indeed of an illustrious family, but, by a variety of untoward events, had been reduced to such poverty that the energy of his character succumbed beneath it, and he ceased to bestir himself in the world, or to care for the retrieval of his fortunes. By courtesy of his creditors, there still remained in his possession a small remnant of his patrimony; and, upon the income arising from this, he managed, by means of a rigorous economy, to procure the necessaries of life, without troubling himself about its superfluities. Books, indeed, were his sole luxuries, and in Paris these are easily obtained. (107–8)[1]

This initial description presents Dupin not as a powerful agent but, on the contrary, as a victim of "untoward events" who is "reduced," who "succumbed," who "ceased." The paragraph's second sentence charts a dulling of Dupin's social luster and a diminution of his energy as he retires from "the world" and its concerns. Ceasing to "care for the retrieval of his fortunes" and to "troubl[e] himself about [life's] superfluities," he withdraws from the demands of the material to inhabit, as it were, a mental landscape. Over the next three paragraphs, the narrator develops this theme of withdrawal, depicting his meeting Dupin; their choice, as their common abode, of "a time-eaten and grotesque mansion, long deserted through superstitions . . . and tottering to its fall in a retired and desolate portion of the Faubourg St. Germain" (108); and the nature of their life together:

> Our seclusion was perfect. We admitted no visitors. Indeed the locality of our retirement had been carefully kept a secret from my own former associates; and it had been many years since Dupin had ceased to know or be known in Paris. We existed within ourselves alone. (108)

Their devotion to darkness, which they "counterfeit" during the day by closing "all the massy shutters" (108), appears only to enforce their separation from the *real* world and, consequently, their attachment to "dreams—reading, writing, or conversing" (108).

This early characterization of the withdrawn and speculative Dupin functions almost as an alibi for the detective, as evidence that he is not present or implicated in the actual world where crime occurs. Dupin's involvement in "dreams" or representations —"reading, writing, or conversing"— seems to guarantee his distance from the world and thus his unprejudiced and innocent perspective upon its affairs. Although those familiar with Caleb Williams are apt to be suspicious of another *innocent* reader, here the story appears less concerned with critiquing the detective than with defining his analytic sensibility. Even if we note that Dupin's narrative hunger is not satisfied with books and that he reads people as well, our identification with the investigator is not likely to be significantly disturbed: the boundary between good detective and bad criminal still seems comfortably intact. The quest for "the same very rare and very remarkable volume" that brings the narrator and Dupin into "closer communion" (108) becomes an image for the readerly and writerly enterprise of the detective, who seeks to uncover the hidden story of the crime. Indeed, the story consistently depicts Dupin's investigatory skills in terms of the linked activities of reading and writing that fashion an unseen story. Just as from a few slim clues Dupin "retrace[s] the course of [the narrator's] meditations" and highlights the "larger links of [that narrative] chain" (110), so from the skimpiest of fragments Dupin linguistically constructs his explanatory narrative of the murders in the Rue Morgue. As Dupin remarks, " 'Upon these two words [*"mon Dieu!"*] . . . I have mainly built my hopes of a full solution of the riddle' " (129).

The impression that Dupin, like the withdrawn reader with her book, exists apart from the world is further developed by the conduct and description of the investigation. In detective fiction the crucial *action*—the crime—usually occurs offstage, and thus much of the story unfolds as a kind of *inaction*, as a meditation on the absent event. This abstraction is especially pronounced in "The Murders in the Rue Morgue," where, in the space of the missing action, the reader encounters first, the textual responses of the reporters and second, the speculations of Dupin. Indeed, the bookish and physically inactive Dupin seems quite content in inhabiting this imaginative region where he studies newspaper accounts, consults Cuvier, and even pens an advertisement for *Le Monde*, an ingenious energy-saving strategy which brings the sailor to the figurative armchair of the detective. One should not forget, of course, that Dupin does exert himself in visiting the house of the murdered women, but even here the physicality of the excursion is muted. Not only does the crime scene become another scene of reading as Dupin "scrutinize[s] every thing" (119), but the visit, which is just briefly sketched by the narrator, is then filtered further by Dupin who returns to it in the course of his explanations. Here the initial physical journey is reconstituted as part of a speculative journey: " 'Let us now transport ourselves, in fancy, to this chamber. What shall we first seek here?' " (122). " 'Let us now revert to the interior of the room. Let us survey the appearances here' " (126). With such instructions, Dupin guides the narrator (and, by implication, the reader) through that explicitly imaginative landscape into which the *real* has seemingly disappeared.

In retracing the mental steps he has taken in solving the "riddle" (129) of the murders in the Rue Morgue, Dupin displays how he plays the *game* of investigation. Indeed, the analogy between detection and game-playing (which Dickens and Doyle will also develop and which is now a commonplace of detective fiction) emerges in the story's first paragraph, where the narrator describes the "enjoyment" derived from analysis:

> As the strong man exults in his physical ability, delighting in such exercises as call his muscles into action, so glories the analyst in that

> moral activity which *disentangles*. He derives pleasure from even the most trivial occupations bringing his talent into play. He is fond of enigmas, of conundrums, of hieroglyphics. . . . (105)

The narrator then extends the list of "occupations" which provide "pleasure" and "play" for the analyst to include the games of draughts (105–6) and whist (106–7) and, by implication, the puzzle of crime itself. Hence Dupin, in suggesting that they examine "these murders," avows that an "'inquiry will afford us amusement,'" before acknowledging more worldly obligations: "'and, besides, Le Bon [the unjustly accused] once rendered me a service for which I am not ungrateful'" (119).

Yet even as such game-playing seems to become an additional sign of the detective's aloofness and his preoccupation with the abstract, it also registers the detective's particular form of social interaction with the world. For the detective's pleasure depends not simply upon opponents he can engage but especially upon opponents he can defeat. Certainly, if the detective takes on only the puzzle of the crime's mysterious clues, his pleasure, like the investigating reader's, seems relatively private. But the detective also obtains a more public pleasure by egoistically imposing his power upon, for example, the author of the mystery. Here Dupin controls the sailor, who is first lured into the figurative prison of the detective's room and then manipulated into divulging the full story of the murders. Similarly, Dupin imposes his power upon any detective who might presume to solve the mystery before him. Of course, his chief rival is the Prefect of Police whom, as Dupin remarks, he is "'satisfied with having defeated . . . in his own castle'" (135). But one might also wonder if Dupin considers even his companion as a rival of sorts, and if, like Bucket and Holmes, he enjoys witnessing the effects of his narration on his immediate audience. For Dupin, successful detection means gaining control of the hidden story of the crime, a control that he demonstrates to his companion by making him submit to the detective's explanations. Dupin directs his friend's passage towards the solution, making him not only marvel at the detective's ingenuity but also suffer the nervous trauma that attends certain narrative revelations. The friend, whom Dupin subjects to his storytelling, "stared at the speaker in mute astonishment" (120); "felt a creeping of the flesh" (128); was "completely unnerved" (128). Thus a gap develops between the composed and controlling Dupin and the disempowered listener, a relationship not entirely dissimilar to that which the detective forges with his ostensible opponent, the sailor. Although the sailor is forcefully manipulated by the text of the advertisement and thus absorbed by the plot that Dupin concocts, the sailor also experiences, like the listening companion, a subtler form of management as his narrative expectations are shockingly thwarted. Anticipating that his orangutan is about to be returned, the sailor suddenly finds himself the subject of a murder inquiry, an astounding turn of events that leaves him "trembling violently" and speechless; his "original boldness of bearing was all gone" (132).[2]

In other words, Dupin's very act of revealing his solution becomes an assertion of power, as the detective-storyteller triumphs over his enervated victims. Indeed, the detective who had seemed to stand apart from the world begins to emerge as a character of the world, engaged in social relationships that soothe his ego and please him with power. Of course, even as one critiques this other Dupin, one must also acknowledge the text's more explicit depiction of Dupin as the detective-hero, who brilliantly overturns the dangerous misinterpretations of the *official* police. For it is certainly Dupin's analytic and writerly power—his ability to provide a "narration of the circumstances" (135)—that effects Le Bon's release and thus counteracts the police's misapplied power. Yet even here where Dupin's storytelling is most appealing—seeming to free rather than to oppress—one might retain some skepticism. One might question if Dupin's solution, which absolves everyone from motive and guilt, is merely a matter of liberating innocence and truth; one might wonder if the detective's power inheres not only in what he can (positively) uncover but also in what he can (more negatively) conceal.

☾

Detection, as a novel such as *The Moonstone* will amply illustrate, often seems more concerned with proving innocence than with proving guilt. In Collins's novel detection works to restore the tainted reputations of not only particular individuals but also the entire community by uncovering the guilty party. To find the criminal, then, is by implication to find a scapegoat, who in this ritual of cleansing and legitimizing is burdened with society's guilt and then sacrificed.[3] In "The Murders in the Rue Morgue," however, the establishment of innocence and social legitimacy unfolds so successfully that no guilty party needs to be apprehended. Indeed, the story's title, which mirrors the reporters' and police's belief that the killings reflect human motive, proves ironic. Dupin illustrates the 'startling absence of motive in a murder so singularly atrocious' (127), and in attributing the brutal deeds to an orangutan proclaims the innocence of not only the sailor but the human species as well.

Detection's strategy of displacing guilt onto *the other* had seemed implicit in the depositions of the "witnesses," who, Dupin notes, consistently described "'the shrill voice . . . as that *of a foreigner*. Each is sure that it was not the voice of one of his own countrymen. Each likens it—not to the voice of an individual of any nation with whose language he is conversant—but the converse'" (121). But Dupin himself ambitiously goes a step further in shifting the blame onto an orangutan, which (as if to compound Dupin's talent of displacement) supposedly can't be blamed because it is only fulfilling its natural identity as an animal. The narrator, who is instructed to read Cuvier's "account of the large fulvous Ourang-

Outang of the East Indian Islands," observes that the "gigantic stature, the prodigious strength and activity, the wild ferocity and the imitative propensities of these mammalia are sufficiently well known to all" (129).[4] While "'the police are confounded by . . . the atrocity of the murder,'" Dupin manages to reconcile the "'*outré* character'" (120) of the killings—that which seems to cry out for justice—with the *natural* state of affairs. Nothing improper, transgressive, or unnatural has happened: the investigation is closed.

Yet does Dupin's solution entirely satisfy the reader? Do Dupin's efforts to naturalize and legitimize behavior raise any suspicions? Do we find more than the obvious irony in the final words of the story, spoken by the authorial Dupin as he brings the narrative of his case to a close? "'I like [the Prefect] especially for one master stroke of cant, by which he has attained his reputation for ingenuity, I mean the way he has *"de nier ce qui est, et d'expliquer ce qui n'est pas"*'"(135). At the end of a paragraph in which he celebrates and constructs his superiority over his rival, Dupin concludes with this statement of false praise that, in a further twist of irony, becomes a sort of true praise. For has not the great detective himself denied or concealed a part of the truth in developing his solution? I'm not disputing Dupin's contention that an orangutan killed the two women; I'm objecting instead to the effect and possible purpose of his solution, which endorses society's innocence and thus seems to conceal the moral crimes at the heart of the story.

For example, left uncommented upon in Dupin's efforts to describe an unmotivated crime is the money-making motive of the sailor, who captures the orangutan and brings it to Paris. We read that the sailor's "ultimate design was to sell it" (133), and, indeed, despite the animal's temporary escape and the ensuing bloodshed, that plan is eventually fulfilled: "It was subsequently caught by the owner himself, who obtained for it a very large sum at the *Jardin des Plantes*" (135). Thus this project of procuring profit brackets the violence in the Rue Morgue, reducing the killings to an unfortunate consequence of a financial enterprise that is left unquestioned and uncontested. Rather than seriously grappling with this origin and cause of bloodshed, Dupin hurriedly dismisses the issue, assuring the sailor of his lack of responsibility: " 'I perfectly well know that you are innocent of the atrocities in the Rue Morgue. . . . You have done nothing which you could have avoided—nothing, certainly, which renders you culpable' " (132). With such words Dupin in effect sanctions the plan of the sailor and the apparent injustice of its bloodstained but successful completion. At this point, Dupin's detection reveals its limitations, skirting the difficult moral issues involving the sailor's actions: seeking the tidy resolution, the investigation disregards the sailor's journey into the interior of Borneo, his capture of the orangutan, his removal of it from its natural habitat to Paris, and, generally, his effort to dominate the animal by means of a whip.

Why does Dupin's detective-storytelling overlook the sailor's motives and actions? Certainly, one could argue that detectives have no right to interfere with matters beyond their purview, and that therefore Dupin correctly confines himself to legal offenses. Yet one could also contend that the sailor's use of control and domination is not entirely unlike Dupin's own employment of power, and that confronting the former would mean confronting the latter. In other words, in shielding the sailor, Dupin protects himself. Dupin avoids facing his own invasions of private spaces, intrusions that suggestively align the detective with not only the sailor, who violates the space of the orangutan, but also the supposed criminal, who invades the private space of the two women and murders them in their own home.

As the horror inspired by the killings in the Rue Morgue indicates, society values privacy; and so, it initially seems, does Dupin, who goes so far as to withdraw from the world itself in his pursuit of seclusion. Yet even as Dupin prizes his own privacy—a disposition that would seem to place him on the side of the victims, the two women who "'lived an exceedingly retired life'" (114)—he is constantly trespassing upon the personal territory of others. Indeed, this contradictory character who, the narrator reports, "had ceased to know or be known in Paris" (108), knows a great deal. For example, when the accounts of the murders appear in the newspapers, Dupin knows two of the principals: the accused Le Bon and G—, the Prefect of Police (119).[5] Of course, Dupin's knowledge is not surprising, given his nocturnal habit of watching the city. During the day, Dupin and the narrator conceal themselves within their "grotesque mansion" (108), but at night they sally "forth into the streets, arm in arm, continuing the topics of the day, or roaming far and wide until a late hour, seeking, amid the wild lights and shadows of the populous city, that infinity of mental excitement which quiet observation can afford" (109). Rather than keeping to himself, the rambling Dupin violates the privacy of others, whom he subjects to "quiet observation" in his effort to extract the "mental excitement" he craves. While the detective's dangerous appetites will be drawn more explicitly in Dickens's *Bleak House*, even here we glimpse the detective as a threatening figure who ventures forth at night like a vampire, seeking to appease his hunger for "eager delight" and "pleasure" (109).

The narrator reports that Dupin "boasted to me, with a low chuckling laugh, that most men, in respect to himself, wore windows in their bosoms, and was wont to follow up such assertions by direct and very startling proofs of his intimate knowledge of my own" (109). This boast represents Dupin as peering inside and also imaginatively entering the private sanctum of the individual; additionally, the image of "windows" subtly links Dupin's intrusions with that of the orangutan who passes through a window into the chamber of Madame and Mademoiselle L'Espanaye. In the conclusion Dupin will brag that he is "'satisfied with having defeated [the Prefect] in his own castle'" (135), a remark that more clearly reveals how the invasive act functions as an assertion of power. Investigation offers Dupin the figurative opportunity to extend his dominion, whether by usurping the role of the Prefect, who can only vainly comment on "the propriety of every person minding his own business" (135); or by "fathom[ing the] soul" (110) of the narrator in the story's beginning. In giving voice to "the course of [the narrator's] meditations" (110), Dupin undermines his friend's independent status. He occupies the narrator's mind, just as later, in the investigation proper, he inhabits the character of the sailor.

Of course, it is this ability to project himself into the mind of his opponent that allows Dupin (and later Holmes) to triumph consistently in the game of detection. As the narrator explains, "Deprived of ordinary resources, the analyst throws himself into the spirit of his opponent, identifies himself therewith, and not unfrequently sees thus, at a glance, the sole methods (sometimes indeed absurdly simple ones) by which he may seduce into error or hurry into miscalculation" (106). John Douglas, one of the most influential figures in modern detection, cites this passage in *Mindhunter: Inside the FBI's Elite Serial Crime Unit*. Writing with Mark Olshaker, Douglas suggests that the "antecedents" of the FBI's work in criminal profiling "actually . . . go back to crime fiction more than crime fact," and that "the amateur detective hero of . . . 'The Murders in the Rue Morgue' may have been history's first behavioral profiler. This story may also represent the first use of a proactive technique by the profiler to flush out an unknown subject and vindicate an innocent man imprisoned for the killings."[6] But despite the brilliance of Poe's and Dupin's techniques, these intrusions into the minds of others remain bothersome; they seem to reproduce on a psychological plane the violations that criminals perform on a physical level. Imagining the possible reaction of the sailor to the advertisement, Dupin adopts the inner voice of his opponent (130–31), reducing him to the subordinate position of a character within the detective's plot. When the sailor appears, in confirmation of the detective's theory, Dupin completes his victory by acquiring the remainder of the sailor's secrets and, in a sense, the remainder of his independence. The passing of "information" becomes a passing of "power" as the sailor accedes to Dupin's demand for "'all the information in your power about these murders in the Rue Morgue'" (132). Thus Dupin presumes to assert his authorial control. But, significantly, he extends that power over not only seemingly legitimate targets, like the sailor, but also seemingly innocent subjects, like the narrator, whom the detective likewise investigates and explains.

If Dupin doesn't wish to emphasize the darker dimension of his own quest for power, he is unlikely to examine seriously the sailor's story. For the sailor's account more clearly reveals the cruelty and dangerous consequences that proceed from the effort to control another being. Described as an "excursion of pleasure," the passage "into the interior" of Borneo (132) and thus into the orangutan's own habitat functions, like Dupin's invasive practices, to gratify the explorer. The sailor attains power by capturing the orangutan, and then he maintains his control by confining it (a tactic that echoes Dupin's imprisonment of the sailor) and by applying his whip. Yet the orangutan does not docilely accept this new arrangement of dominator and dominated:

> Returning home from some sailors' frolic on the night, or rather in the morning of the murder, he found the beast occupying his own bed-room, into which it had broken from a closet adjoining, where it had been, as was thought, securely confined. Razor in hand, and fully lathered, it was sitting before a looking-glass, attempting the operation of shaving, in which it had no doubt previously watched its master through the key-hole of the closet. (133)

The "imitative" (129) animal rebels against its subservient position by breaking out of its assigned "closet," "occupying" the sailor's "own bed-room," and performing the sailor's activity of shaving. Suddenly, then, their positions become reversed. The sailor is displaced from his role as master, and in a desperate attempt to retrieve it he uses his whip, setting in motion the horrifying chain of events that follow.

The sailor's story seems to suggest that tension, friction, and ultimately violence result from the violation of personal space. Of course, the sailor acts brutally from the start in forcibly removing the orangutan from the jungle; but violence is not publicly acknowledged until it visibly affects humans. Although the sailor denies the orangutan's independence, he is not prepared for that animal's challenge of his own autonomy nor for that collapse of personal boundaries that follows the animal's rebellion and escape. Thus the intrusion into the women's room is not simply an accident—an event disconnected from significant causes—but a consequence of that erosion of privacy initiated by the sailor. Denied a place of its own, the orangutan finds sanctuary where it can. Yet in constructing his solution, Dupin treats the killings as an accident; in his authoritative position as detective-storyteller, he wields the power of declaring what is acceptable behavior and what is not. If the hidden story of "The Murders in the Rue Morgue" portrays the dangerous breakdown of boundaries between individual beings, the public story of the solution attempts to cover over that incriminating evidence. Indeed, in shaping his narrative, the detective imposes his own boundaries, which, in excluding what doesn't belong to the story, powerfully defend the detective's own privacy and thus his public presentation of himself.

"The Mystery of Marie Rogêt"

When Dupin reappears at the beginning of "The Mystery of Marie Rogêt" (1842–43), the narrating friend once again emphasizes the detective's reclusive personality:

> Upon the winding up of the tragedy involved in the deaths of Madame L'Espanaye and her daughter, the Chevalier dismissed the

> affair at once from his attention, and relapsed into his old habits of moody reverie. Prone, at all times, to abstraction, I readily fell in with his humor; and, continuing to occupy our chambers in the Faubourg Saint Germain, we gave the Future to the winds, and slumbered tranquilly in the Present, weaving the dull world around us into dreams. (143)

As the narrator points out, however, their "dreams were not altogether uninterrupted" (143), and "the cases were not few in which attempt was made to engage [Dupin's] services at the Prefecture" (144). Yet when a specific interruption does occur, in the form of the Prefect's request for assistance with the case of Marie Rogêt, the life of Dupin seems to undergo little change. The "researches which had absorbed [his] whole attention" (146) before the Prefect's arrival are merely exchanged for a new subject of inquiry. Indeed, rather than forcing Dupin into the world, detection again seems to be the perfect pastime for this man of abstraction. Even more so than in the earlier mystery story, the detective inhabits a period of non-action, for this story of investigation excludes not only (necessarily) what comes before (the hidden events comprising Marie's disappearance) but also what comes after (the apprehension of the supposed criminal based on the application of Dupin's ideas). In place of the latter, Poe constructs a fictional note from the story's editors, who remark that they "have taken the liberty of here omitting, from the MSS. placed in our hands, such portion as details the *following up* of the apparently slight clew obtained by Dupin" (184). Although the note states "that the result desired was brought to pass" (184), our experience is of the speculation itself, of Dupin as a creative reader who attempts to re-present the missing action through his analysis of textual information.

Dupin, then, seems effectively distanced from the *real*, for not only does he seek to construct his own representation of the lost action of the past but he attempts to do so by examining other textual responses to the hidden event, namely the Prefecture's "full report of all the evidence elicited" (147) and the many newspaper stories on the case. Yet just as this emphasis on textuality underlines Dupin's seclusion, it also works to expose the worldly motives that drive storytelling and detection. By closely studying the reporters' efforts to illuminate the mystery, Dupin manages not only to undercut the authority of these detectives but also to cast suspicion generally upon the storytelling enterprise. Dupin advises us "'that, in general, it is the object of our newspapers rather to create a sensation—to make a point—than to further the cause of truth'" (155). But what, the story subtly asks, are the motives underlying and possibly corrupting the other acts of detection? If we can accuse the reporters of writing for money, of fanning the sensation of Marie's disappearance in order to create more excitement and attract more readers, we can charge Dupin with a similar offense. For he works for the financial compensation offered by the Prefect, a reward, Dupin reminds the narrator, that will only be forthcoming if the dead woman is, in fact, Marie Rogêt:

> "If, dating our inquiries from the body found, and thence tracing a murderer, we yet discover this body to be that of some other individual than Marie; or, if starting from the living Marie, we find her, yet find her unassassinated—in either case we lose our labor; since it is Monsieur G— with whom we have to deal. For our own purpose, therefore, if not for the purpose of justice, it is indispensable that our first step should be the determination of the identity of the corpse with the Marie Rogêt who is missing." (155)

Here Dupin connects "labor" to monetary reward, and notes a possible discrepancy between his own "purpose" and the "purpose of justice." As for the Prefect, G—, he too is compelled by worldly motives, seeking to preserve his "reputation," his "honor" (146), and, by implication, the position that earns him money. As he informs Dupin and the narrator, "The eyes of the public were upon him; and there was really no sacrifice which he would not be willing to make for the development of the mystery" (146).

Like "The Murders in the Rue Morgue," "The Mystery of Marie Rogêt" subverts the image of the detective as withdrawn, innocent, and objective by exposing his entanglement in the world and thus his motives for storytelling. Honor, for example, drives the Prefect whose "sacrifice," ironically, is evident in his dishonorable willingness to accept the credit ensuing from Dupin's detection. But honor also figures in the motivation of Dupin, who seems preoccupied with defining his brilliance both for others and for himself. Although not obviously in the "eyes of the public" (146) like G——, Dupin nevertheless performs for a sizable audience that may include the entire Parisian police and its emissaries for whom "the name of Dupin had grown into a household word" (143), as well as those who read his friend's account (which, significantly, contains Dupin's own account) of his exploits. Dupin, however, seems most intent on affecting his immediate group comprised of his friend, rival detectives, and the criminal. Of course in this mystery, which omits the apprehension of the criminal and thus the glorious climax of the detective's case, Dupin's opportunity to triumph is necessarily limited. Dupin's power is implicit in the remark (by the story's fictional editors) that "the Prefect fulfilled punctually, although with reluctance, the terms of his compact with the Chevalier" (184), but that power appears most explicitly in his dissection of the reporters' stories. In dismantling their arguments, Dupin figuratively deposes these rival detectives, clearing the way for the establishment of his own theory and thus his own supremacy.

Dupin defeats the reporters by exposing their general designs of making money as well as their particular designs of bending reason and evidence to support their arguments. Yet, as we have seen, the charge of design may also rebound upon Dupin, who detects to affirm his own sense of himself—to witness his power as it is reflected by both the reward he obtains and the impression he makes upon his audience. In "The Mystery of Marie Rogêt" that audience consists primarily of the narrator, who feels the mastery of Dupin and who witnesses once again that detective's authorial presumption of entering the minds of the characters in his mystery. Dupin adopts the voice of Marie Rogêt as he describes her intention of never returning home (171),[7] and he occupies the character of "the murderer" as he relates that figure's actions after the crime (183–84). Although Dupin acknowledges in each instance that he is speculating, his imaginative account nevertheless attains a sinister authority. Dupin, after all, is the detective who constructs the story of what happened, and in this truncated mystery there is no opportunity for the criminal to contest Dupin's rendition of events. In other words, Dupin becomes an unchallenged storyteller who egotistically transforms the *real* figures of the mystery into characters who inhabit his authorial vision.

In his attempt to construct a story, the detective typically functions as a figure for the author of detective fiction. That connection, however, becomes particularly intriguing in "The Mystery of Marie Rogêt," where Poe, in his efforts to solve the *real* mystery of the disappearance of Mary Rogers, likewise becomes a figure for his detective. Moreover, in his presumption of knowing the people involved in the *real* case, Poe seems to embody the least appealing traits of his fictional character. By considering the evidence available to him and crafting the parallel story of Marie Rogêt, Poe "believe[d]" (he wrote on 4 June 1842) that he had "*indicated the assassin* in a manner which will give renewed impetus to the investigation."[8] But, as is now well known, that narrative design, which would have established "the man of dark complexion" (182) as the murderer, encountered a significant obstacle five months later. Suddenly, before Poe's third and final installment was printed in the *Ladies' Companion,* the mystery was apparently solved and Poe's explanation overturned. According to the New York *Tribune* of 18 November 1842, Mrs. Loss (who became Madame Deluc in Poe's tale) made a deathbed confession of certain "facts":

> On the Sunday of Miss Rogers [*sic*] disappearance [Mary] came to [Mrs. Loss's] house from this city in company with a young physician who undertook to procure for her a premature delivery.—While in the hands of her physician she died and a consultation was then held as to the disposal of her body. It was finally taken at night by the son of Mrs. Loss and sunk in the river where it was found.[9]

Although the accumulation of rumors and reports surrounding Mrs. Loss's death did not amount to "proof," as John Walsh observes, "it all added up to the strong probability that Mary Rogers had died in an abortion attempt and had not been throttled, as Poe's story concluded, by a naval officer or any other individual."[10] What was Poe to do, faced with a setback that seemed to symbolize the very limitations of the detective-storyteller's art? Walsh, in his investigation of that question, suggests that Poe "persuaded [William] Snowden [of the *Ladies' Companion*] to postpone the third segment of *Marie Roget* [from the January] to the February issue so that changes could be made in it." Furthermore, Walsh demonstrates how Poe, in preparing the story for republication in his *Tales* (1845), "made fifteen small, almost undetectable changes in the story, all of which definitely accommodate the possibility of an abortion death at the inn of Madame Deluc . . . —and then he added detailed footnotes so that it would appear he had been entirely correct from the start!"[11] Poe's confronting of the abortion theory, then, foregrounds the fabrications to which the detective-storyteller may resort in pursuit of an authoritative narrative and, especially, the gap between speculation and reality. Indeed, in Poe, like Dupin, we glimpse the power of the detective who may so easily misinterpret the evidence, distort the truth, and thus effectively reduce others to the position of characters in a plotted fiction.

"The Purloined Letter"

The power that derives from the telling of another's story figures as a prominent concern in early detective fiction. *Caleb Williams* examines a struggle between oppressive storytellers, while the Dupin stories focus upon the authority residing in one clearly masterful character. In the first two Dupin stories that authority (of defining character and drawing the boundaries between what is to be revealed and concealed) arises from the detective's ostensible ability to explain what happened. By contrast, the narrative opportunity offered to Dupin in the third and final story, "The Purloined Letter" (1844), may initially seem limited, for here the identity of the criminal and the details of the theft are known from the beginning. Where, then, is the story that the detective seeks to control? Actually, the concealed narrative in this mystery is represented by the purloined letter itself which, in its illumination of the illicit behavior of a royal lady, becomes a document of personal and political importance that the criminal desires to exploit and that the lady desires to suppress. Thus Poe's tale of the document's retrieval, with Dupin pitted against the Minister who has taken figurative possession of the lady's secret life, explicitly engages that issue of narrative control that underlies detective fiction. In "The Purloined Letter" the goal of detection becomes literally the acquisition of the hidden story.

The notion of the otherworldly detective reappears in "The Purloined Letter," which opens, like the two previous stories, with Dupin in seclusion: "At Paris, just after dark one gusty evening in the autumn of 18—, I was enjoying the twofold luxury of meditation and a meerschaum, in company with my friend C. Auguste Dupin, in his little back library, or book-closet. . . " (200). Once again, however, details of the story will subvert the image of the withdrawn and objective detective, so that Dupin emerges not so much as one uncovering and thus reflecting reality as one actively shaping it. In the earlier stories the detective's creative impact upon the world appears most obviously in Dupin's search for power, which can be registered only in social relationships based on his authority and others' vulnerability. Similarly, in "The Purloined Letter," the desire for power motivates Dupin as he triumphs over his narrating friend, the criminal, and the Prefect, who again relinquishes a reward to his rival.[12] But in this case the detective's work not only informs his relationships and produces profit, it also becomes politically significant as Dupin " 'act[s] as a partisan of the lady concerned' " (215). In Dupin's turning of the tables so that the Minister, who has so long controlled the lady, is unwittingly in her power, Poe's tale emphatically illustrates the worldly influence that derives from managing the hidden story.

Such mistrust of the detective's power necessarily unsettles the comforting conclusion which detective fiction supposedly offers. Of course, when the investigator's stealing of the letter from the Minister's hotel mimics the Minister's theft from the royal boudoir, suspicion only intensifies and the opposition between detective and criminal begins to erode. In the criminal's act, as described by G—, we now recognize that usurpation of personal narrative commonly practiced by Dupin:

> "At this juncture enters the Minister D—. His lynx eye immediately perceives the paper, recognises the handwriting of the address, observes the confusion of the personage addressed, and fathoms her secret. After some business transactions, hurried through in his ordinary manner, he produces a letter somewhat similar to the one in question, opens it, pretends to read it, and then places it in close juxtaposition to the other. Again he converses, for some fifteen minutes, upon the public affairs. At length, in taking leave, he takes also from the table the letter to which he had no claim." (202)

Here the criminal becomes a "lynx eye" and, in his actions, very much a private eye as he brilliantly reads the clues of "handwriting" and "confusion," and detects the underlying narrative. Like the visionary Dupin, who "fathom[s the] soul" (110) of the narrator at the beginning of "The Murders in the Rue Morgue," the Minister "fathoms her secret." The Minister gains "ascendancy over the illustrious personage" (202) through acts of containment: first, he mentally encompasses her inner life in his deduction; then, he absorbs her into the mini-drama involving his feigned reading of his own letter; and finally, he takes figurative possession of her in claiming the letter that contains her secrets.

In many detective fictions, the offense represents an unjust assertion of authorial power as the criminal assumes control of another's story and deploys it for his own ends. We glimpse such oppressive authorship, for example, in the machinations of Falkland, who frames Caleb; of Stapleton, who designs the hounding of Sir Charles and Sir Henry Baskerville; and of Count Fosco and Sir Percival Glyde, who conspire to plot the life of Laura in Collins's *The Woman in White* (1860). In "The Purloined Letter" the Minister interprets the clues, constructs the lady's secret life, and then absorbs that story into his plot of blackmail. If the crime, however, occurs as storytelling, how do we respond to the solution, which likewise arises as storytelling and likewise presupposes a controlling power? Is detection, as characterized in this tale of the twice-stolen letter, really a kind of thievery in which the investigator fulfills his own motives by apprehending and containing the criminal plot, and thus appropriating the entire story? Poe's story engages these questions by underlining the similarity of the detective and his antagonist, the suggestively named D——, whose Dupin-like analytic talents enable him to control not only the lady but also the police, whose actions he foresees. The Minister's power, like Dupin's, derives from intellect, imagination, and the strategic deployment of what he knows; furthermore, both are poets (204), a characteristic indicative of their skill with language and hence their adeptness in fashioning stories.[13]

To counteract the plotting of the criminal, the detective must be equipped with considerable narrative skill. Dickens's Bucket and Doyle's Holmes, for example, exhibit superb counterplotting, while the first-person narrator-detectives of *Caleb Williams* and *The Moonstone* literally write narratives to establish records of the *truth* that will overturn ostensibly false versions. In "The Purloined Letter," Dupin displays his power early in his verbal teasing of the Prefect. Cautioned that the Prefect would probably lose his job if it became known that he had confided the substance of his current case to anyone, the narrator tells G— to " 'Proceed,' " while Dupin archly responds, " 'Or not' " (201). Dupin strikes again when the Prefect, concluding his description of the purloining of the letter, remarks that the lady,

> "driven to despair, . . . committed the matter to me."
>
> "Than whom," said Dupin, amid a perfect whirlwind of smoke, "no more sagacious agent could, I suppose, be desired, or even imagined."
>
> "You flatter me," replied the Prefect, "but it is possible that some such opinion may have been entertained." (202–3)

Here Dupin's intellectual superiority is indicated both by his ironic wit, which diminishes the Prefect, and by that rival's apparent failure to detect more than the surface meaning of the utterance. These minor verbal flourishes occur, of course, during the Prefect's first visit, when Dupin has yet to begin his investigation; when the Prefect next appears, he is subjected to a more extensive display of Dupin's facility with language and narrative.

If Dupin were merely interested in the recovery of the letter, he could have volunteered to accompany the police on one of their searches of the Minister's hotel. But for Dupin recovering the letter is inextricably connected to exerting power over both the criminal and the Prefect, and therefore he acts alone. Dupin sets in motion his own secret plan, which emerges as the Prefect's first visit closes. In advising the Prefect to "'make a thorough research of the premises,'" Dupin ensures his rival's mounting frustration, and in procuring " 'an accurate description of the letter' " (206), Dupin obtains information useful to his own private search.

Thus the detective prepares for the scene that unfolds when the baffled Prefect returns and, prodded by Dupin, pronounces,

> "I would *really* give fifty thousand francs to any one who would aid me in the matter."
>
> "In that case," replied Dupin, opening a drawer, and producing a check-book, "you may as well fill me up a check for the amount mentioned. When you have signed it, I will hand you the letter."
>
> I was astounded. The Prefect appeared absolutely thunder-stricken. For some minutes he remained speechless and motionless, looking incredulously at my friend with open mouth, and eyes that seemed starting from their sockets; then, apparently recovering himself in some measure, he seized a pen, and after several pauses and vacant stares, finally filled up and signed a check for fifty thousand francs, and handed it across the table to Dupin. The latter examined it carefully and deposited it in his pocket-book; then, unlocking an *escritoire*, took thence a letter and gave it to the Prefect. This functionary grasped it in a perfect agony of joy, opened it with a trembling hand, cast a rapid glance at its contents, and then, scrambling and struggling to the door, rushed at length unceremoniously from the room and from the house, without having uttered a syllable since Dupin had requested him to fill up the check. (207)

Even as we acknowledge Poe's narrative ability to startle us, our attention shifts to the scene's figurative author, Dupin, who has crafted this unexpected turn of events with great care. For this sensational moment is not a casual product of sudden invention but the result of Dupin's patient cultivation of the seeds sown at the end of the Prefect's first visit. Deliberately, Dupin fashions a dramatic revelation that forcefully impresses his power, even upon his own companion who, intentionally kept in the dark, is now "astounded." Primarily, however, the scene affects the Prefect, whose "thunder-stricken" appearance testifies to Dupin's ability to plot the action in an artful way. The same gap between controlling author and victimized audience that emerges in "The Murders in the Rue Morgue" opens here. Just as the sailor of the former story is stunned into submission by the unexpected when he answers Dupin's advertisement (132), so here the Prefect is left "speechless" and emotionally and physically overwrought. Whereas the Prefect now becomes a powerless and comic figure, deprived in his excitement of both his voice and his control over his own body, Dupin clearly assumes his position of authority, directing his rival in the signing of the check and, with that official's departure, "enter[ing] into some explanations" (207). Indeed, at this point Dupin asserts his mastery over the story, for his figurative shaping of the action symbolized by this scene is succeeded by his explicit narration in which, for the tale's remaining pages, he linguistically controls what happens.

The conclusion in which the brilliant detective relaxes at the end of the mystery and explains how he reached his solution would become a common feature of detective fiction. Doyle titles Holmes's summation in the final chapter of *The Hound of the Baskervilles* "A Retrospection," a term that signifies the new position that the detective assumes toward his case. For mystery, as long as it prevails, is a condition of the here and now, whereas solution belongs to the past, to the time when the detective is no longer contained by the puzzling events authored by the criminal but has moved outside them to a position of retrospective understanding. In "The Purloined Letter," Dupin's ability to narrate an explanation represents his authorial containment of the Minister's plot, a design which, in turn, had encircled both the royal lady and the police. Dupin wins this contest of storytellers because he constructs the most encompassing plot, and he does so because he identifies his "'intellect with that of his opponent'" (208). This technique, by which the child "'won all the marbles of the school'" (208), is employed in the self-gratifying games of both the Minister and Dupin as they transform opponents existing outside their plots into manipulable characters existing inside. As Dupin explains, such identification enables the Minister to counteract the designs of the police, for he "'could not have failed to anticipate . . .

the waylayings to which he was subjected,'" and he "'must have foreseen . . . the secret investigations of his premises'" (212). Of course, this very description of the "'train of thought [that] would necessarily pass through the mind of the Minister'" (212) becomes an illustration of Dupin's own strategy of identifying and thereby disempowering the thinking of his opponent.

Viewing detection as a form of artistic expression, like his successors Bucket and Holmes, Dupin cunningly weaves his counterplot:

> "I prepared myself with a pair of green spectacles, and called one fine morning, quite by accident, at the Ministerial hotel. I found D— at home, yawning, lounging, and dawdling, as usual, and pretending to be in the last extremity of *ennui*. He is, perhaps, the most really energetic human being now alive—but that is only when nobody sees him." (213)

Dupin combats the Minister's pretense of passiveness by assuming a role of his own.[14] Though Dupin has "prepared" for his visit, he acts as if he has arrived by "accident," and though he "'cautiously and thoroughly surveyed the apartment,'" he pretends to be resting "'weak eyes'" and focusing "'only upon the conversation of [his] host'" (213). Indeed, Dupin outperforms the Minister (whose physical pose and disguised letter are seen through) and, in his second visit, fully incorporates that opponent into his own design. By scripting the drama that unfolds in the street below, Dupin constructs the Minister as the spectator who involuntarily "'rushed to a casement, threw it open, and looked out'" (215). At that instant of distraction, Dupin not only pockets the letter but replaces it with a "'carefully prepared'" facsimile (215) so that his counterplot remains invisible. Consequently, the Minister will continue to behave as if he is still an independent agent, not knowing that now, as an actor in Dupin's drama, he is performing a role that ensures "'his political destruction'" (215).

Each of these stories invites us to consider Dupin as a detective whose very seclusion would seem to ensure his objective perspective upon the world. And each of these stories proceeds to undermine that notion of *innocent* vision, exposing Dupin's motives and thus his entanglement in the social world he presumes to explicate. In the Dupin stories the detective emerges not as the criminal's polar opposite but as an ambiguous figure who shares that transgressor's desire for control. Just as the criminal wields power in enacting the unexplained events of the mystery, so the successful detective asserts greater power in absorbing the criminal and his hidden story into a more comprehensive narrative. What this fiction stages, then, is a contest for storytelling supremacy as the investigator pits himself against both criminal and rival detectives in his bid to tell the story—to craft the twists and turns of narrative, to define characters, to display his authority. More explicitly than the other stories, "The Purloined Letter" portrays both this struggle for narrative control and the worldly motives that guide the detective. For despite Dupin's otherworldly veneer, his attempt to acquire the letter and its secret story is driven, for example, by his "'political prepossessions'" (215) and the lure of financial reward. Yet Dupin's ambition is even more personal than that. Most simply, he is fulfilling his need to express his power to others—to his friend to whom he narrates his dramatic account; to the Prefect who formally recognizes his power with the check of fifty thousand francs; and to the Minister who had once done him "'an evil turn'" (216), and who, of course, wouldn't recognize "'the identity of the person who had outwitted him'" (216) without the telltale clue that Dupin carefully provides. Like Odysseus taunting Polyphemos,[15] Dupin cannot slip away unnoticed from the scene of his triumph, but must leave the signature of his handwriting, the subtle but powerful impression of himself.

THREE

"The Narrow Track of Blood"

Detection and Storytelling in *Bleak House*

THE CHARM OF the Dupin stories rests partly in their depiction of detection as an exciting but comfortable form of reading. In these stories the violence of crime may entertain—providing the titillating subject matter for speculation and analysis—but not endanger. Crime is pushed offstage, into the past, and confronts Dupin only as a set of clues, an aesthetic puzzle that may be solved pleasurably. Here, then, the detective exists innocently apart from the world's contagion: at least that is the notion that the Dupin stories halfheartedly indulge. In *Bleak House* (1853), however, there is no fostering of this illusion of the detective as aloof and privileged onlooker; indeed, there is no sense of an outside to a world whose overwhelming physicality is so brilliantly rendered in the novel's opening pages. In Dickens's novel detection is clearly of the world and of the people: it has become the habitual practice of a guilt-ridden society, whose members detect in order to exert control over others and themselves.

☾

The following passage from Dickens's description of Tulkinghorn's funeral procession in chapter 53 of *Bleak House,* entitled "The Track," juxtaposes two of the novel's major detectives:

> Contrast enough between Mr. Tulkinghorn shut up in his dark carriage, and Mr. Bucket shut up in his. Between the immeasurable track of space beyond the little wound that has thrown the one into the fixed sleep which jolts so heavily over the stones of the streets, and the narrow track of blood which keeps the other in the watchful state expressed in every hair of his head! (628)[1]

The lawyer Tulkinghorn, who had been busily unearthing the secret history of Lady Dedlock, is now a murder victim and, ironically, a subject of inquiry. Death "has thrown [him] into the fixed sleep"; life with its promise of flux and flow has lapsed into rigidity. Furthermore, Bucket attempts to cast the spent vein of Tulkinghorn's life into an analogously rigid form; he energetically pursues "the narrow track of blood" in an effort to define its origins and ends and thus its narrative boundaries. He desires, of course, to follow the bloody track to the murderer and thus to possess the entire story of the crime, but he also craves more localized authority over the individual—a power expressed, for example, as he assembles the case against Hortense, and here as he proceeds to make the lawyer his own, figuratively writing, even ingesting, the "track of blood" that vitalizes and maintains him in "the watchful state expressed in every hair of his head."

The investigator's authorial role as one who pieces together and hence "writes" the story of the crime is a motif common to both the criticism and practice of detective fiction. Even the earliest masters of the form conceive of the detective's work as the definition of an intelligible narrative. In *A Study in Scarlet* (1887)

Sherlock Holmes offers this explanation to Watson: " 'There's the scarlet thread of murder running through the colourless skein of life, and our duty is to unravel it, and isolate it, and expose every inch of it.' "[2] Similarly, in *The Woman in White* (1860), Wilkie Collins's amateur detective, Walter Hartright, seeks to determine the complete narrative line that will release the protagonists from entrapping mystery. Like Franklin Blake of Collins's *The Moonstone,* Hartright is significantly both a principal writer and the editor of the linked narratives that form the story, roles that underline the authorial nature of detection. As Hartright writes late in his final narrative, "Two more events remain to be added to the chain, before it reaches fairly from the outset of the story to the close."[3]

In *Bleak House* the metaphor is neither a "thread" nor a "chain" but a "narrow track of blood," an image that preserves the sense of a narrative line but also more powerfully evokes the physical notion of tracking and pursuit. Indeed, in Dickens's novel, where several characters—Jo, Gridley, Nemo, and Lady Dedlock—are hounded even to death, detection is relished by its various practitioners as if the scrutiny and hunting down of others promised to satisfy some primitive hunger. Not unlike the figurative cannibalism of Vholes, the "man-eating" (483) lawyer who feeds upon his client Richard Carstone, the detective derives nourishment from the subjects of his investigation. Bucket is invigorated by the blood of Tulkinghorn; and later as his investigation nears completion he pronounces satisfaction: "'It is a beautiful case'" (632), a statement suggesting forgetfulness of individual suffering and enthusiasm for the story he has constructed. The greed here is not for flesh nor for financial sustenance; it is rather, as Tulkinghorn implies when he tells Lady Dedlock that her discovered past is " 'my secret' " and not " 'your secret' " (581), a more sinister kind of consumption—a desire for the narrative and thus for the private identity of another.

In chapter 33, entitled "Interlopers," Dickens embodies this hunger for secrets[4] in the two reporters who had previously investigated Nemo's mysterious death and who now reappear to "write with ravenous little pens" (403) the even more sensational story of Krook's demise. As "public chroniclers" (133) intruding into the private worlds of others, the journalists and their devouring pens characterize that insatiable demand for stories that motivates the novel's many inquisitive characters. Why are so many of the novel's characters depicted as investigators in quest of intimate knowledge? Perhaps the main reason is that Dickens's characters fear self-exposure—and their own guilt—and turn instead to probing the inner lives of others. Such detection is a soothing distraction, and yet at the same time it proceeds as if it were the crucial search for hidden meaning, for the concealed knowledge that will confer stability and perhaps even identity upon the self. Lacking (and dreading) a defining sense of themselves, these detectives compensate by attempting to read and write the objects of their detection; they attempt to nourish their own spiritual hunger by feeding on the identities of others.

That the detected are also numerous reflects the novel's guilt-ridden society in which the habit of scrutiny is so ingrained that an actual crime is not necessary to call it forth. Indeed, more than two-thirds of the novel passes before Tulkinghorn is murdered, yet in those pages we read, for example, of the pursuit of Jo by Bucket, of Esther by Guppy, of Nemo and Lady Dedlock by Tulkinghorn, and of Mr. Snagsby by Mrs. Snagsby. Suspicion of an underlying corruption motivates the policeman who "begins to push at doors; to try fastenings; to be suspicious of bundles; and to administer his beat, on the hypothesis that every one is either robbing, or being robbed" (393). The presumption of guilt operates apart from obvious evidence of crime and seems to emerge instead from a sense of humankind's innate depravity. Thus "the narrow track of blood" is not simply the spilled blood linking the murderer and his victim but, more pervasively, it is the bloodline of family that contaminates the individual by linking him or her to the "sins of the fathers."[5]

The burden of the past and of its potentially debilitating influence is powerfully represented by the prolonged Chancery case of Jarndyce and Jarndyce. Esther terms the case "the fatal blight" (289); Mr. Jarndyce refers to it as "the family curse" (302); and Richard Carstone describes how he " 'was born into this unfinished contention with all its chances and changes, and it began to unsettle [him] before [he] quite knew the difference between a suit at law and a suit of clothes' " (288). Jarndyce and Jarndyce is an inescapable consequence of birth, an "unfinished contention," an inherited story that entraps and unsettles, challenging Richard's ability to chart his life freely and thus express a distinct, individual identity. Just as Richard is implicated in an inherited story, the Dedlock cousins seem physically and psychologically tainted by their ancestry:

> The rest of the cousins are ladies and gentlemen of various ages and capacities; the major part, amiable and sensible, and likely to have done well enough in life if they could have overcome their cousinship; as it is, they are almost all a little worsted by it, and lounge in purposeless and listless paths, and seem to be quite as much at a loss how to dispose of themselves, as anybody else can be how to dispose of them. (348)

These examples suggest a conception of impurity that is inherent in the human condition and is passed from generation to generation —a sort of original sin.[6] In this light Mr. Jarndyce's fervent philanthropy seems partly a compensatory reaction to his own sense of depravity and culpability; and Esther's selfless activity seems driven by intimations of her own guilt.[7]

As a child Esther grows up with feelings of guilt, which are given special definition by the charge of her godmother on her birthday:[8]

> "Your mother, Esther, is your disgrace, and you were hers. The time will come—and soon enough—when you will understand this better, and will feel it too, as no one save a woman can. I have forgiven her"; but her face did not relent; "the wrong she did to me, and I say no more of it, though it was greater than you will ever know—than any one will ever know, but I, the sufferer. For yourself, unfortunate girl, orphaned and degraded from the first of these evil anniversaries, pray daily that the sins of others be not visited upon your head, according to what is written. Forget your mother, and leave all other people to forget her who will do her unhappy child that greatest kindness. Now, go!" (19)

The "godmother's" advice for Esther is not particularly consistent; she advises her to keep her illegitimate origins uppermost in her mind by "pray[ing] daily" that the sins of the parents "are not visited" upon the child, and yet she also recommends that Esther "forget" her mother. Indeed, the godmother's own actions embrace this contradiction. She expresses denial in that she " 'had bred [Esther] in secrecy from her birth, had blotted out all trace of her existence' " (213); and yet she simultaneously reveals acute acceptance of the illegitimate birth in her obsessive efforts to erase Esther's familial identity. For in stating that "'your mother, Esther, is your disgrace, and you were hers,'" the godmother reads Esther as the sign and embodiment of sin, even as a clue that must be carefully hidden.

According to Esther's godmother, "'submission, self-denial, diligent work, are the preparations for a life begun with such a shadow on it'" (19); and Esther repeats this prescription in the intentions she often confides to her doll:

> . . . I would try, as hard as ever I could, to repair the fault I had been born with (of which I confusedly felt guilty and yet innocent), and would strive as I grew up to be industrious, contented, and kind-hearted, and to do some good to some one, and win some love to myself if I could. I hope it is not self-indulgent to shed these tears as I think of it. (20)

Significantly for her own chances of maturing into a healthy adult, Esther feels not only guilty of "the fault" but also innocent. Her sense of innocence emboldens her to recognize the goodness and importance of her self, an awareness represented by her very narrating of the story in which she assumes a central place. Yet her guilt compels her to voice distrust about telling her own story. In iterating her purpose to her doll, Esther chooses selflessness rather than self-proclamation; and even in her retrospective writing she is wary of the possible self-indulgence of the tears she sheds in revisiting the early part of her history. Just as Esther's godmother had attempted to blot "out all trace of her existence," the guilty Esther continues the process of erasing the self and "the fault" it represents by attempting to be self-less—that is, by following the recommended practice of "submission and self-denial."

One could say that the guilty, such as Esther, internalize detection. Adhering to a doctrine of self-denial, they rigorously police themselves, and through such scrutiny keep the flawed self—the criminal—in check. Esther attempts to repress what she regards as her inherited, tainted self; and later, when she is disfigured by illness, Esther views her transformation in similar terms of concealment: "I felt . . . a burst of gratitude to the providence of God that I was so changed as that I never could disgrace her [Esther's mother] by any trace of likeness; as that nobody could ever now look at me, and look at her, and remotely think of any near tie between us" (449). Esther's thankful reaction is typically selfless—selfless in the concern for her mother, who is the object of Tulkinghorn's detection, and selfless in accepting the necessity to obscure the "trace of likeness" and thus hide her own ineradicable familial identity. Esther's guilt inheres in the very fact that she (the product of an illicit sexual union) exists, and thus her plight is highly symbolic, expressive of that inheritance that plagues the characters of *Bleak House*. Indeed, characters seem to contain within themselves the very evidence that might incriminate them, and thus they seek to conceal those traces whether they have obvious reason to do so or not. Lady Dedlock, in her flight in the final portion of the novel, disguises herself so as better to elude her pursuers, who circulate a written "description" of her (675). But, as we have seen, Esther also seeks to hide herself, and those professionally involved with the law make it a practice not to expose themselves unnecessarily. Guppy tells Esther: " 'Being in the law, I have learnt the habit of not committing myself in writing' " (359), a notion with which Mr. Bucket concurs; for "he often sees damaging letters produced in evidence, and has occasion to reflect that it was a green thing to write them" (629).

The reluctance to write emerges from the notion that it is dangerous to express oneself—dangerous because, at root, one may be guilty. And handwriting is not only a vehicle for self-expression but also a set of personal characteristics that functions as a sign of identity. One of the major lines of inquiry in the novel begins when Tulkinghorn registers Lady Dedlock's reaction to a legal document copied by a law-writer. We eventually discover that the handwriting belongs to Lady Dedlock's lover, Captain Hawdon; but this figure is first introduced to the reader (and to the investigating Mr. Tulkinghorn) as Nemo, a dead man on a bed in a shabby room over Krook's shop. As Tulkinghorn explains, " 'Nemo is Latin for no one' " (121); "the lonely figure on the bed, whose path in life has lain through five-and-forty years, lies there, with no more track behind him, that any one can trace, than a deserted infant" (131). While detectives will eventually "trace" his "track," Nemo reveals such an extreme desire for concealment that he completes the erasure of himself in death, thus establishing "his pretensions to his name by becoming indeed No one" (126).

The extreme fear of discovery and definition drives Nemo and later Lady Dedlock toward suicidal acts of obliteration. Nemo dies "of an over-dose of opium" (126), while Lady Dedlock flees from Tulkinghorn into "the shrill frosty wind" (667), oppressed with the "terrible impression . . . that from this pursuer, living or dead—obdurate and imperturbable before her in his well-remembered shape, or not more obdurate and imperturbable in his coffin-bed,—there is no escape but in death. Hunted, she flies" (666). In the midst of her flight Lady Dedlock writes to Esther: "'I have done all I could to be lost. I shall be soon forgotten so, and shall disgrace him [Sir Leicester Dedlock] least. I have nothing about me by which I can be recognised'" (710). The exposure and disgrace, which Tulkinghorn (and the whole apparatus of detection) threatens, drive Lady Dedlock to this final effacement, an act that seems to complete the "conscience-stricken" policing of self that she has so long sustained. In one sense her death suggests her decision—of hiding, of avoiding further humiliation, of making a final gesture of control over a life story that is quickly falling into the hands of others. But in another sense even that small freedom is denied her. She does not destroy her self but has that self destroyed by others. For, as she imagines: "Her name is in these many mouths, her husband knows his wrongs, her shame will be published—may be spreading while she thinks about it" (665). This intimation seems to eradicate any remaining hope of sustaining her identity, an impression of an independent self that is based on interior depths that are private and unknown. Thus Lady Dedlock no longer has a self to erase because, in her mind, she has become the property of others—constructed in the gossip passed from mouth to mouth and in the sensational journalism published in newspapers. She does not escape and hide in death but is hounded to that final destination where, her "name . . . in these many mouths," she is devoured by a hungry public.

The individual's right to privacy is constantly threatened in *Bleak House*. Boythorn's war with Sir Leicester Dedlock over "the disputed thoroughfare" (764) translates this concern about the autonomous self into a debate over private property. Elsewhere we read of Jenny's husband, the poor brickmaker, protesting against intrusions into his home: "'I'm not partial to gentlefolks coming into my place. . . . I let their places be, and it's curious they can't let my place be. There'd be a pretty shine made if I was to go a wisitin *them,* I think'" (683-84). Property becomes an extension or representation of one's self, and unwanted intrusions become acts of violation. The privacy of one's property and one's self are conjoined in a description of what Sir Leicester possibly sees in his empty room after Bucket has summed up the case and arrested Mademoiselle Hortense: "The green, green woods of Chesney Wold, the noble house, the pictures of his forefathers, strangers defacing them, officers of police coarsely handling his most precious heir-looms, thousands of fingers pointing at him, thousands of faces sneering at him" (653). As Dickens's sentence unwinds, we move from the estate's surrounding property, inside the "noble house" and to the smaller, portable objects—"the pictures of his forefathers," and "his most precious heir-looms"—that also represent Sir Leicester Dedlock. This inward movement enacts an invasion of self, of the proud and vulnerable identity that is constituted by this inheritance. Now "strangers" reign in the house, "defacing" and thus redefining his pictures; his possessions are "coarsely" handled by "officers of police" and thus degraded to fit within their investigatory scheme. Essentially this sentence hunts down Sir Leicester—the concluding "him"—until he is ringed about by "thousands of fingers pointing at him, thousands of faces sneering at him." In this nightmare vision, his authority over his life (suggested by the initial descriptive terms of the emphatically "green" and thus majestic woods, and the "noble" house) has been replaced by the authority of the strangers, the police, and finally the public throng who effectively rewrite him by imposing those sordid views suggested by their "pointing" and "sneering."

Bleak House depicts the public's enthusiasm for stories and the threat that such an appetite engenders. Confronted by Tulkinghorn's revelation that he possesses her secret story, Lady Dedlock asks her torturer: "'Is it the town-talk yet? Is it chalked upon the walls and cried in the streets?' " (508). Her vision, like her husband's, of the public's articulation and thus appropriation of one's private life suggests the vulnerability of identity in the novel. Characters lack faith in a personal identity when their selves seem constructed both by an impersonal past and an impersonal public. When an individual seems to exist as a copy of the past, and can be re-copied by others in the present, trust in a centered, unique self dwindles and the individual potentially becomes one among a confusing proliferation of copies. Indeed, in its preoccupation with the way an individual is represented by gossip, paintings, physical descriptions, and handwriting, *Bleak House* generates a profusion of copies that questions the primacy of the supposed original. Dickens's description of "the Dedlocks of the past [who] doze in their picture-frames" (572) grotesquely conflates the *actual* people with the paintings of them. Mr. Guppy visiting Chesney Wold early in the novel encounters a " 'portrait of the present Lady Dedlock' " that " 'is considered a perfect likeness,' " and proclaims " 'how well I know that picture' " (82). As we discover, the similarity between Lady Dedlock and her picture is extended to Esther, who inherits her mother's features. And Esther, in turn, is suggestively described as an " 'image . . . imprinted on my art' " (361) by Guppy, who, obsessed with this possible familial connection, defines Esther in terms of her shared characteristics; later when those similarities are destroyed by illness, Guppy reports to his friend Mr. Weevle (alias Tony Jobling) that the " 'image is shattered' " (490).

Weevle himself also worships representations, namely "a choice collection of copper-plate impressions from that truly national work, The Divinities of Albion, or Galaxy Gallery of British Beauty, representing ladies of title and fashion in every variety of smirk that art, combined with capital, is capable of producing" (256). As a fan, Weevle is one of the many whose craving for the latest gossip supports that journalism that hounds the fashionable set. Earlier in the novel we read of a "brilliant and distinguished circle"

(144) who "have come to pass a January week or two at Chesney Wold, and which the fashionable intelligence, a mighty hunter before the Lord, hunts with a keen scent, from their breaking cover at the Court of St. James's to their being run down to Death" (144). In his absorption with these glamorous lives (as they are refigured in the public consciousness), Weevle—and by analogy the reader—is implicated in the voracious pursuit that undermines and eventually eradicates privacy and individuality. Weevle desires to know the fashionable and achieves an intimacy, but at second hand. His familiarity extends to copies—to the portraits and their further representation in newspapers and gossip—but somehow this contact seems sufficient:

> To borrow yesterday's paper from the Sol's Arms of an evening, and read about the brilliant and distinguished meteors that are shooting across the fashionable sky in every direction, is unspeakable consolation to him. To know what member of what brilliant and distinguished circle accomplished the brilliant and distinguished feat of joining it yesterday, or contemplates the no less brilliant and distinguished feat of leaving it to-morrow, gives him a thrill of joy. To be informed what the Galaxy Gallery of British Beauty is about, and means to be about, and what Galaxy marriages are on the tapis, and what Galaxy rumours are in circulation, is to become acquainted with the most glorious destinies of mankind. Mr. Weevle reverts from this intelligence, to the Galaxy portraits implicated; and seems to know the originals, and to be known of them. (256)

The passage itself seems to distinguish between the copies (which, described hyperbolically as "brilliant and distinguished meteors," are explicitly fictitious) and "the originals"; but Weevle, like so many other characters in the novel, blurs this division. In Weevle's confusion the "portraits" to which he "reverts" seem real and are "implicated," and "the originals" themselves lose their distinctiveness and primacy—for Weevle, at the height of his delusion, "seems to know the originals, and to be known of them." Strangely, Weevle's intimacy with these fictions seems to center him in a significant relationship, to identify him as being "known." The information about the fashionable nourishes Weevle, providing him with "unspeakable consolation" and "a thrill of joy," lifting him from his comparative insignificance and squalor to an acquaintance "with the most glorious destinies of mankind."

The presence of a determining past and of a defining present (of detectives and journalists) threatens and questions the self's ability to be itself. Reproductions in the form of paintings, published stories, and verbal accounts jostle for space with the supposed original; even handwriting and physical descriptions become substitutes for the self in the detective's effort to track down and thereby usurp individuality.[9] These latter signs are employed to identify and control people—in other words, to deny them their independence and privacy and to subject them to external definitions. In pursuit of Jo, Bucket and Snagsby descend into Tom-all-Alone's and then conduct their search by repeatedly describing the boy to the inhabitants of the area until he is found. Similarly, "a description" (this time written out and "then copied" [675]) functions in Bucket's search for Lady Dedlock; but here Lady Dedlock frustrates the pursuit because she understands her identity as an image and disguises herself. Yet the significant point is that detection does not have to be successful to effectively determine its prey; the very threat of pursuit, especially as it coalesces around the figure of Tulkinghorn, drives Lady Dedlock to guilty flight and to the very embracing of that criminal identity that she seeks to avoid.

The coercive influence of detection, then, is not strictly related to the skills of its best practitioners, who at key moments in the novel prove fallible: Tulkinghorn fails to discern that he should not go home on the night of his murder (582-83); and Bucket fails to perceive the fugitive Lady Dedlock when "he mounts a high tower in his mind, and looks out far and wide" (673). Yet suggestions of these detectives' omnipresence—and, by implication, omniscience—pervade the novel. Mr. Tulkinghorn "walks into Chesney Wold as if it were next door to his chambers, and returns to his chambers as if he had never been out of Lincoln's Inn Fields" (514); or, "Time and place cannot bind Mr. Bucket. Like man in the abstract, he is here to-day and gone to-morrow—but, very unlike man indeed, he is here again the next day" (626). These descriptions by the third-person narrator are not literal but impressionistic renderings of Tulkinghorn's and Bucket's powers, suggesting how particular acts of investigation may engender an oppressive sense of widespread surveillance.[10] Tulkinghorn is not omnipresent but to Lady Dedlock he seems to be: "Always at hand. Haunting every place. No relief or security from him for a moment" (575). Similarly, the image of Bucket pursues Jo, who (as Woodcourt explains) " 'in his ignorance . . . believes this person to be everywhere, and cognisant of everything' " (563). The very notion of detection quickens feelings of guilt and fear in both Jo, the most ignorant and innocent, and Lady Dedlock, whose own past becomes criminalized, at least in part, because it is secret and thus subject to exposure.

In a world beset by intrusive detection and storytelling, identity perhaps inheres most essentially in what is secreted in the darkest, most disgraceful corner of the self. In extreme instances—the final days of Lady Dedlock and Nemo—characters seem to identify themselves fully with this last refuge of the personal and the private as they obsessively attempt to elude both literal and imagined pursuers. For the most part, however, the common anxieties of guilt and the desire for concealment are managed more effectively, as characters seek to dissociate themselves from their latent sense of sin. Instead of being policed by others—and thus defined as the "criminal" in flight from the "respectable" forces of inquiry—such characters police themselves, repressing a transgressive self and thereby affirming a law-abiding identity.[11] This practice of self-control is most emphatically represented by Tulkinghorn, who, with his "expressionless mask," is "his own client . . . and will never betray himself" (147). In other words, Tulkinghorn embodies a system of regulation, being in himself both the oppressive law and the client with dangerous secrets.

Perhaps more important, characters distance themselves from the fearful and private world of the self by indulging a distracting interest in the world of society. Some choose to detect others and thus manage to disfigure (i.e., disguise) themselves psychologically. Instead of being constructed by guilt (and by the investigations conducted by others), such a character decides to define and determine the subjects of his own inquiries. Such a detective separates the sense of self from the sense of personal criminality and powerlessness and assumes an authoritative and more comfortable position on the right side of the law. Others reap similar rewards by practicing a less strenuous form of investigation. Weevle hunts the fashionable through networks of gossip and sensational journalism, and Dickens's readers by implication satisfy analogous cravings by pursuing the narrative's mysteries and devouring its secrets. Finally, some choose philanthropy, which, at its most intrusive, resembles the detective enterprise of shaping or narrating lives. Esther and Mr. Jarndyce not only seek concealment (or selflessness) in beneficent acts but also psychologically assume new definitions as persons who determine for the better the lives of others.

Each of these methods of distraction generates a common satisfaction, as the fear of victimization is suppressed by the exhilaration of molding the lives of others. The pressure that Weevle alone can exert upon others may seem negligible, but he is a part of the largely nameless public that hounds—and articulates the identities of—the famous and infamous. Obviously some distinctions should be made between an instrument of good such as Mr.

Jarndyce and (in George's words) "'a slow-torturing kind of man'" (566) like Tulkinghorn; but curiously, even Mr. Jarndyce's philanthropy veers toward manipulation as he designs Esther's life with Woodcourt. Less problematic are the coercive tactics of a philanthropist like Mrs. Pardiggle, who, Esther reports, "had such a mechanical way of taking possession of people." She "pulled out a good book, as if it were a constable's staff, and took the whole family into custody. I mean into religious custody, of course; but she really did it, as if she were an inexorable moral Policeman carrying them all off to a station-house" (99). The apt comparison between Mrs. Pardiggle and the police emphasizes the regulatory power that both attempt to wield. While Mrs. Pardiggle specializes in moral bullying, the police employ both physical power—in moving Jo on and in incarcerating George—and psychological weaponry. For instance, Bucket enforces submission not only by his very presence (as an image of surveillance) but also by his ability to construct a case, a narrative designed to control the subjects of his investigation.

Bucket's authorial control is much in evidence in *Bleak House,* particularly when he unveils the story of Tulkinghorn's murder. "From the expression of his face" when he meets Sir Leicester Dedlock alone in the baronet's library, Bucket "might be a famous whist-player for a large stake . . . with the game in his hand, but with a high reputation involved in his playing his hand out to the last card, in a masterly way" (636). This comparison to a "whist-player" underlines Bucket's power, which has simplified the human players and complexities of the mystery into a very manageable handful of cards that are to be deployed not only successfully but also artistically. While Bucket's energetic management of the bewildering world of *Bleak House* can be both reassuring[12] and, at times, comically delightful, his detection nevertheless jeopardizes individuality. The game-playing analogy, which Bucket himself also uses in referring to possible "move[s] on the board" (638), suggests the chilling reductiveness of his interpretations;[13] and his pride in his aesthetic sense as he dramatically unfolds his explanatory narrative implies an oppressive egotism that likewise threatens the self-expression of others. When Grandfather Smallweed presumes to intrude onto Bucket's professional ground and questions his handling of the inquiry, Bucket responds in a tone that subdues his foolhardy challenger and with words that confidently reassert his artistic competence:

> "I am damned if I am a going to have my case spoilt, or interfered with, or anticipated by so much as half a second of time, by any human being in creation. *You* want more pains-taking and search-making? *You* do? Do you see this hand, and do you think that *I* don't know the right time to stretch it out, and put it on the arm that fired that shot?" (643)

In his jealous protection of his "case" and his rejection of interference "by any human being in creation," Bucket seems to declare his own superiority—indeed his own position as a sort of rival creator, who controls time down to the half-second and who merely needs to stretch forth his wondrous hand to transform the chaos of mystery into the order of solution. After Grandfather Smallweed and his group depart, Bucket supports his claim of knowing the exact time to arrest the criminal. As he "refers to his watch," Bucket announces to Sir Leicester, his astonished audience of one: "'The party to be apprehended is now in this house . . . and I'm about to take her into custody in your presence'" (646). The entrance of the murderer, Hortense, a moment later confirms Bucket's and, of course, Dickens's creative ability to manage events in time and thus to construct the sensational moments of narrative itself.

Admittedly, detection is Bucket's job, and a murderess deserves to have her freedom constrained. But in a novel preoccupied with the ravenous character and dangerous consequences of investigation, Bucket's activities cannot escape criticism. Even his bluff familiarity, which he extends to most who cross his path, emerges as a strategy of authorial control, as he essentially tells people who they are:

> "Yes! and lookee here, Mr. Snagsby," resumes Bucket, taking him aside by the arm, tapping him familiarly on the breast, and speaking in a confidential tone. "You're a man of the world, you know, and a man of business, and a man of sense. That's what you are." (276)

With such intimacy and insinuation, Bucket initiates a one-sided conversation that seeks to define Snagsby's character and thus the role he shall play for the detective. Later, in pursuit of Gridley, Bucket employs similar conversational tactics on George and indeed begins with the same definition—" 'You're a man of the world' " (311)—which, we see, is not really a statement of George's general practicality in the world at large but rather of his specific utility within the realm that is Bucket's.[14]

These snapshots of Bucket's "conversational powers" (594) significantly illustrate his facility with language and thus forecast his adeptness in shaping stories.[15] And those stories are finally determined through the detective's activity of tracking, the pursuit that so often in *Bleak House* concludes with a dead body. The discovery of the corpse of Lady Dedlock, for example, suggests the success of the detection instigated by Tulkinghorn and completed by Bucket. She has been found physically (and therefore can no longer elude the forces that seek to control her); and she has been found out, indeed to such an extent that she no longer has any life or identity of her own. She has been chased to her final end, to that point of closure that allows Bucket (and by analogy the voracious reader) to possess her story. Although Bucket's authorial confidence is momentarily shaken as he loses the fugitive's track—the narrative thread as it were—he quickly claims ascendancy again. To Esther he seems "an excited and quite different man," as he exclaims " 'I've got it!' " and announces his decision to reverse direction. He tells Esther: " 'You called her Jenny, didn't you? I'll follow her' " (689). Bucket simultaneously discerns the trick of the exchanged clothes and regains his writerly balance, withholding this crucial secret in service to the suspenseful integrity of his story. Earlier, Bucket—displaying an artistry similar to Poe's Dupin—had delayed naming the murderer in order to orchestrate the startling entrance of Hortense. Just as he then wasted little worry on poor Sir Leicester's nerves, here he overlooks "the suspense and anxiety" afflicting Esther as, in her mind, they leave her "mother farther and farther behind every minute" (703). For the anguish Esther feels and the shocking revelation that awaits her as she discovers her mother in Jenny's clothes are, to Bucket, tributes to his power—to his knowledge as a detective and to his manipulative strategies as a storyteller.

Walter Benjamin writes that

> the novel is significant . . . not because it presents someone else's fate to us, perhaps didactically, but because this stranger's fate by virtue of the flame which consumes it yields us the warmth which we never draw from our own fate. What draws the reader to the novel is the hope of warming his shivering life with a death he reads about.[16]

Because the reader exists in the midst of his own life, it lacks the completion and rounding significance provided by death. Denied this consoling meaning, the reader seeks vicarious compensation, finding characters in the novel form whose lives have been concluded and thus rendered meaningful by a literal or "figurative death." Benjamin's powerful argument about novel reading has implications not only for assessing our own interest in the deaths of *Bleak House* but also for understanding how the novel's characters find satisfaction in the literal and metaphorical deaths of others. Perhaps many of these characters possess such a ravenous desire to define others, to position them in the meshes of a story, even to trace an individual's life's track to its final expiration, because they lack and dread such fixity in their own lives. Characters want the rigors of such murderous meaning imposed on others, not on themselves; they prefer to believe in a vague notion of their own freedom, that they are not determined by the guilt of inheritance, their past, or the members of their society. Consequently, they live vicariously, keeping their own lives strictly private and rather empty. In a sense, such a character wants an identity without having to have an identity, to be known without being known. Strangely enough, such selfhood seems to be attained in *Bleak House* by the many who feed off the lives and stories of others. Weevle, for example, in his pursuit of the Galaxy Gallery of British Beauty, "seems to know the originals, and to be known of them" (256). Knowledge makes him feel known and nourishes him within an artificial network of intimacy. A similar notion of identity is fashioned by the gossip that attends the flight of Lady Dedlock; as Dickens remarks: "Not to know that there is something wrong at the Dedlocks' is to augur yourself unknown" (690). Gossip and the stories that investigation constructs maintain the safety of one's privacy, yet they stimulate a sense of identity through the shared cultural experience and the even closer sharing that seems to emerge from an emotional nearness to the principals involved.

In *Bleak House* Dickens presents a world rife with secrets and the hunger for them, a world whose spirit is masterfully rendered in the depiction of the Smallweeds' search through Krook's rag and bottle shop:

> all day, do they all remain there until nine at night, . . . rummaging and searching, digging, delving, and diving among the treasures of the late lamented. What those treasures are, they keep so secret, that the court is maddened. In its delirium it imagines guineas pour-

> ing out of teapots, crown-pieces overflowing punch-bowls, old chairs and mattresses stuffed with Bank of England notes. (491)

The craving for secrets expands ringlike, from the greedy investigation of the Smallweeds within the privacy of the shop; to the hysteria of the court amassed outside, who themselves probe the garbage left for the dustman; to the inquisitiveness of the journalists, "the two gentlemen who write with the ravenous little pens . . . [and] are seen prowling in the neighbourhood" (491); to the fevered anticipation of Dickens's readers. This tension between secrets and detection produces superb storytelling—indeed generates a fictional world in which the quest for, and articulation of, narratives is a dominant activity. But this tension also provides the opportunity for Dickens to interrogate his own sensationalism, to explore the human impulses and desires that underlie the dispositions toward self-concealment and the uncovering of stories. Through his own investigation Dickens reveals the seeds of guilt that shape the consciousness of both the detected and the detectives and that thus engender the dark urgency of his novelistic world.

It is perhaps surprising and certainly noteworthy that in a world dedicated to self-censorship, Esther raises her autobiographical voice. Her disclosure seems an act of courage and self-acceptance, the product of that developing sense of innocence that tells her she is defined neither by her illegitimate past nor by others. "I knew I was as innocent of my birth as a queen of hers" (454), Esther proclaims as she struggles to quell the feelings of guilt that would implicate her in a criminal story and thus deny her the freedom to shape her own life. In telling her own story, Esther claims some authorship over her life and strategically denies others the opportunity of pilfering her secrets and thereby asserting rival ownership. Yet despite her strength, Esther cannot completely transcend the guilt that cripples so many; indeed her self-writing contains a conflict between self-expression and self-denial. The proud and defiant enunciation of self, which the very act of writing suggests, is undermined by currents of doubt. She both exposes and erases, revealing herself for a moment and then retreating behind a mask of coyness. She covers over her own thoughts and, on the final page, veils her own appearance, suggesting but not confirming her beauty. She even attempts to disguise the fact that she is writing autobiography: "As if this narrative were the narrative of *my* life!" (27) she scoffs. But it is, and remarkable though her attempt at telling is, she cannot summon sufficient confidence to narrate herself completely; she cannot fully discard her cloak of selflessness that so ably protects and conceals.

FOUR

The Detection of Innocence in The Moonstone

As *Caleb Williams* and *Bleak House* suggest, the joint activities of detection and story-making may operate not so much to prove another's guilt as to affirm one's own innocence. In Godwin's novel the offensive procedure of detection ultimately becomes a defensive measure: storytelling serves as a means of vindicating one's character. In Dickens's novel the very act of investigating—of aligning oneself with the respectable authority of the law—becomes a technique of evading detection. The way in which detective storytelling functions as a self-interested assertion of innocence emerges most explicitly, however, in Wilkie Collins's *The Moonstone* (1868). The goal of Franklin Blake's investigation of the Moonstone's disappearance is not to determine *who done it* but to prove that Blake himself didn't do it. Blake detects in order to defend his character and to win Rachel back; his inquiry and the book itself climax not in the unmasking of Godfrey Ablewhite as the culprit but in Jennings's experiment, which ostensibly uncovers Blake's innocence. Indeed, in its concern with reputation, Blake's investigation becomes the precursor of that formal construction of narrative designed to protect the "memories of innocent people" (7).[1] This protection and assertion of innocence is the motive for storytelling in *The Moonstone,* a motive actually voiced even earlier, in the "Prologue," where the writer of "a family paper" cautiously narrates the story of John Herncastle's crime in order to defend his own character against misinterpretation and reclaim the "good opinion" of his family.

Although this study focuses on how nineteenth-century detective fiction critiques detection and the construction of narrative, I do not wish to deny the ways in which these texts also endorse the work of the detective. It is not surprising, for example, that an author would feel some affection for a character whose very cleverness in piecing together the criminal story mirrors his own ingenuity in devising plots. As I have suggested, Bucket—and one could cite Dupin and Holmes as well—seems to offer the reader reassurance; in the dark, perplexing world of *Bleak House* he is a guide we would like to trust, a figure whose confident showmanship in unfolding his case reminds us of the authorial mastery of Dickens himself. Franklin Blake of *The Moonstone,* however, is attractive in a different way. As I have remarked elsewhere, Blake's project of determining his innocence may be read as a sincere act of self-determination. Trapped, like the protagonists of each of Collins's major novels, in an oppressive plot he does not control, Blake investigates in order to achieve some authority over the direction of his life. He frees himself from the impersonal plot—symbolized by the legacy of the Moonstone's curse—not only by proving his innocence of the theft (and thus his separation from the inherited story) but also by his very determination to establish his innocence. Unwilling to relinquish his romance with Rachel and to acquiesce to the chain of events set in motion by Colonel Herncastle's will, Blake detects and so figuratively writes his life, bringing it more closely into accordance with his own desires.[2]

Yet even as the novel equates Blake's detection with self-expression, it subverts that identification, suggesting how Blake's investigative writing also functions as self-denial. Like Esther Summerson's autobiography, which is simultaneously an assertion and a negation of self, Blake's writing is contradictory. Ostensibly an act of investigation, of inspecting the world, it reveals a compulsion to limit inquiry and restrict vision; ostensibly an act of self-definition, it reveals a need to suppress the less respectable sides of the self. Thus the detective's shaping of narrative becomes a strategy of self-performance, a means of controlling the information about himself and defending his innocence. Just as the writer of the "Prologue" seems well aware of how his narrative should influence the "decision" (1) and "opinion" (6) of his family, so Blake seems acutely conscious of how his narrative should function in relation to its audience. Indeed, it is the sense of an audience, real or imagined, that controls writing and conduct in *The Moonstone*. The very prospect of judgment—levied by a reader such as "a member of the family reading these pages fifty years hence" (213) or by a more immediate watcher such as a newspaperman, a gossip, or an intimate acquaintance—pushes characters like Blake, Betteredge, and Clack to try to create favorable representations of themselves. In other words, in their very awareness of the possibility of surveillance, these characters internalize that surveillance, monitoring both their behavior and their narrative description of it. Thus the work of discovering and of narrating that investigation becomes a performance in which we view perhaps not so much detection as the evasion of detection, and not so much the uncovering of truth as the attempt to cover it over.

The delicate nature of detection clearly emerges in the family's attempts to maintain its aura of innocence. Of course, the respectability of the family also means the respectability of those individuals who partly derive their identities from membership in the family, and who now rely on the careful detection of Cuff, the "'confidential man'" (183) whose "'professional existence depends on holding [his] tongue'" (187). As Cuff explains, "'I had a family scandal to deal with, which it was my business to keep within the family limits. The less noise made, and the fewer strangers employed to help me, the better'" (187). While Cuff obviously intends to locate the truth, he also intends to suppress it. The emphasis rests on the containment and muzzling (147) of scandal, so that the reputations of the family and its members might be preserved and the division between private and public maintained.

If Cuff and a family member like Blake are ultimately quite different in their conceptions of detection, they resemble one another in their desire to hush things up.[3] For Blake detection involves controlling his image and thus countering the detection of the public who are eager to speculate and to draw narrative conclusions at the hint of any scandal. Indeed, the danger of such "public curiosity" (231) becomes apparent in Clack's narrative when we discover that the family's security has been breached, and, as Rachel suggests, "'Some of our private affairs, at home . . . seem to have got into the newspapers. . . . And some idle people, perfect strangers to us, are trying to trace a connection between what happened at our house in Yorkshire and what has happened since, here in London'" (231). In the latter sentence, Rachel depicts the investigative pastime of strangers who are attempting "to trace a connection" and thus construct a story that will explain mysterious events. Later, Bruff refers to this narrative preoccupation when he acknowledges the suspicions surrounding Godfrey Ablewhite and how "'they're telling a pretty story about that charitable gentleman at my club'" (242). As in *Bleak House*, the public becomes menacing in its hunger for secrets, which compels it not only to violate the privacy of individuals but also, in a sense, to take possession of those individuals by presuming to narrate their identities. " 'I have become the property of the newspapers' " (227), Godfrey informs Lady Verinder and Miss Clack, pretending to downplay his irritation even as he voices the very anxiety about identity and self-control that motivates the family's defensive storytelling.

The power of the public, then, inheres not only in its story-making (through which it assumes a kind of ownership of the individual) but also in its constant watchfulness (through which it forces the individual into self-protective behavior). In *The Moonstone* this system of surveillance becomes particularly oppressive, conducted as it is by professional and non-professional alike. The efforts of Superintendent Seegrave and Sergeant Cuff are supplemented by the work of numerous amateurs, including, obviously, Blake, Bruff, and the young Gooseberry, whose prominent eyes suggest his powers of observation and thus his natural ability as a private eye. The last three stake out the bank when the diamond is withdrawn, just one of many scenes of watching in the novel. Penelope has a ready eye and ear, as does Clack who, for example, secretly witnesses Godfrey's successful proposal to Rachel; and both investigators record their discoveries in their diaries.[4] Rachel, Rosanna and, eventually, Godfrey are watched, and Blake himself becomes the subject of scrutiny in the experiment performed by Jennings. Of course, overarching all of these acts of observation is the mandate of the Brahmins, who are to keep a constant watch upon the Moonstone. According to the legend, Vishnu the Preserver

> commanded that the Moonstone should be watched, from that time forth, by three priests in turn, night and day, to the end of the generations of men. And the Brahmins heard, and bowed before his will. The deity predicted certain disaster to the presumptuous mortal who laid hands on the sacred gem, and to all of his house and name who received it after him. (2)

In this myth of surveillance where "the three guardian priests" even resort to "disguise" (3) in keeping successful watch over the Moonstone, and where punishment ultimately accompanies transgression, we find a narrative expression of the fear of detection that haunts the characters of the novel. Although this anxiety has its roots in the social realities of detectives and gossips, it burgeons into a paranoia in which characters suspect that they are constantly observed and that their slightest misdeeds will be exposed.

Alexander Welsh has argued that the

> nineteenth-century English novel . . . repeatedly dwells on the hero's fear of publicity. . . . [B]eginning with the Waverley Novels of Scott, novels make clear what the rest of the historical record states only imperfectly: namely, that the anxiety of the law-abiding citizen is lest he or she be thought to break the law, or find himself or herself outside the pale of society.[5]

The fear of exposure and expulsion is particularly evident in the world of the detective novel in general and of *The Moonstone* in particular, where the pressure of public inquisitiveness drives both the criminal and the ostensibly innocent into hiding.[6] In other words, Godfrey Ablewhite is not the only character in Collins's novel whose "life had two sides to it" (502). The universal suspicion of being under scrutiny forces characters to perform, to divide themselves between a public persona and a private self, whose compulsions must be censored and repressed. This is not to say that what is hidden is significantly truer than what is publicly visible. Indeed, it is probably because what is unknown seems identifiable to the anxious individual with what remains personal that the private self (like the performative self) becomes unnatural and unreliable. The private self—because it must be hidden—becomes *guilty*, and that which is publicly displayed becomes an advertisement for one's respectable status in the community.

Coordinating the public perception of oneself means controlling and organizing the available information about oneself. And as *The Moonstone,* like Collins's *The Woman in White,* makes clear, a considerable mass of information is potentially available. Constructed as a collection of documents, *The Moonstone* includes the narratives of Betteredge, Clack, Bruff, Blake, and Cuff, the extracts from Jennings's journal, the letter of Rosanna Spearman, the extract from a family paper, and the statements composing the Epilogue. Instead of attempting to obscure its own textuality, the novel self-consciously flaunts it, emphasizing how stories are carefully assembled for particular reasons. Certainly, one of the central reasons seems to be to find out exactly what happened; just as Jennings discovers the coherence underlying Candy's delirious utterances by following " 'the principle which one adopts in putting together a child's "puzzle" ' " (415), so the detective pieces information together to uncover the suppressed story of the crime. But the story-making process is not free of bias, even if the repeated description of the investigation as an "experiment" lends a semblance of scientific rigor to the undertaking.[7] While experimental investigation may reassure the reader, suggesting how incorrect theories are discarded in the process of identifying those that accord with fact and experience, such testing of theories may also unsettle the reader, suggesting the subjective, speculative, and provisional nature of narrative. After all, *The Moonstone* depicts not only the eventual uncovering of the supposed truth but also the many explanations or theories that predate that discovery. Unable to tolerate mystery for long, characters crave explanations, even if they are later rejected or revised. That a skilled and experienced interpreter like Cuff can draw false conclusions about Rachel's guilt should make us doubtful of the general reliability of the narrative patterns that are constantly being formed, and thus, perhaps, sympathetic to the individual's desire to control how he or she is perceived by a story-making public. In constructing his own story, Blake, for example, displays himself as a respectable man:

he makes himself publicly known, and thereby attempts to rid himself of the mystery that would invite speculation and thus subject him to the storytelling of others.

Such self-writing may be understood not so much as an assertion of freedom as an expression of the anxiety that one is not free. The prospect of others' storytelling *forces* one to take control of one's image—to posture and perform—and thus avoid the fate of Jennings, whose reputation is destroyed by rumor and speculation. In a novelistic world where there is no clear relationship between individuals' characters and their reputations, the noble Jennings may be isolated as disreputable and the criminal Ablewhite embraced as an emblem of respectability. Herncastle, for instance, is "avoided by everybody" (33) not because of his past actions but because of *reports* of his past actions, such as the family paper describing his violent theft of the Moonstone. As Betteredge remarks, "There was more than one slur on the Colonel that made people shy of him; but the blot of the Diamond is all I need mention here" (33). Although Herncastle has not been apprehended by the law and imprisoned like Rosanna, he too has a record that labels his identity; rather than manipulating how the public reads him, he is subjected to the dossier of information that is compiled about him.[8]

One of the best illustrations of how control over information equates with power is the criminal career of Godfrey Ablewhite, whose initial success as a thief derives precisely from what he knows that others don't know. On the night when the Moonstone is taken from Rachel's sitting-room, Ablewhite functions as the unseen witness whose perspective most fully encloses the action. According to Cuff's report, Ablewhite "not only detected [Blake] in taking the Diamond out of the drawer—he also detected Miss Verinder, silently watching [Blake] from her bedroom, through her open door" (506–7). While Ablewhite's motives in following the drugged Blake initially seem harmless and perhaps even laudatory—he supposedly wants to prevent an accident—the repeated use of "detected" suggests how his efforts have accidentally accorded him power. As we have seen, a detective detects with the intention of gaining storytelling supremacy. Although the criminal initially attains power in creating his hidden plot, the successful detective asserts his superior power through his ability to read and thus define that inscrutable story: he uncovers buried information, organizes it, and thus eventually absorbs the criminal's plot within his own controlling narrative of explanation. Obviously, as an unintentional act, Ablewhite's detection is quite different, but it still places the discoverer in a position of authority on the periphery of events where, as the ultimate observer, he is differentiated from the characters he watches. Blake and Rachel remain actors in the scene, unaware of its full context, and Ablewhite seems to remain invulnerably outside it, in possession of information from which he can profit. As Ablewhite learns next morning, Blake is "absolutely ignorant" of his actions, including his later delivery of the Moonstone to Ablewhite, and Rachel was "resolved to say nothing. . . . If Mr. Godfrey Ablewhite chose to keep the Diamond, he might do so with perfect impunity" (507).

For the moment Ablewhite assumes a position of power, and he keeps the Moonstone, motivated, of course, by the necessity of speedily acquiring the financial means to conceal his previous crime of defrauding a young gentleman of twenty thousand pounds. But Ablewhite and his secrets become increasingly vulnerable, and soon he is the one contained by the power of information. When he tells the aptly named Luker how he obtained the diamond, Ablewhite falls under the control of the money-lender, whose new knowledge allots him a position of control on the story's periphery. "[C]aught in a trap," Ablewhite is forced to accept the unattractive terms offered by Luker, who, according to Cuff's summation, "didn't profess to know how" the "conversation of that evening would be kept strictly secret" (508) unless he himself had business reasons for keeping it so. Unable to suppress his secrets, Ablewhite gradually relinquishes the management of his life, succumbing to the plots not only of Luker but also of his mistress, who will not consent to his marriage to another until he has "made a handsome provision for her" (509), and of the three Brahmins who kill him in the process of recovering the Moonstone.

Ablewhite's desperate effort to shield his private life and maintain his public persona dramatizes a struggle for self-control that is implicit in the lives of many of the novel's characters. Although other characters may not actually be guilty of crimes, their actions, like Ablewhite's, are informed by the need to meet the scrutiny of others and even themselves with the guise of respectability. In his original "Preface" to the novel (1868), Collins writes that the "attempt made here is to trace the influence of character on circumstances," a claim that seems particularly credible when we consider his characters' preoccupation with their own appearances. Constantly challenged by others' speculations and their own feelings of innate guilt, characters cannot rely on existing identities but must constantly fashion and sustain their reputations in the actions they self-consciously perform. In *The Moonstone,* as in *Caleb Williams,* identity is on trial, and the figurative courtroom is society itself. At the close of his first narrative, Betteredge reverts to the metaphor of the trial that underlies the entire narrative project:

> In this matter of the Moonstone the plan is, not to present reports, but to produce witnesses. I picture to myself a member of the family reading these pages fifty years hence. Lord! what a compliment he will feel it, to be asked to take nothing on hearsay, and to be treated in all respects like a Judge on the bench. (213)

This fictional premise pushes readers toward a recognition of their own implication in the social dynamics of performance and judgment. While most members of such a system will inevitably be compelled to defend their innocence, here the emphasis rests on our roles as judges, deciding the fate of the defendants who will be either included in, or excluded from, the community.

☾

The motif of the trial alerts us to how writing in *The Moonstone* veers away from straightforward reportage to become an instrument of self-defense. The eccentric Betteredge, for instance, attempts to justify his behavior by citing his obedience to the text of *Robinson Crusoe,* which (in Collins's parody of the practice of *sortes biblicae*) he opens at random to find words that will comfort and guide him in the trials of this life.[9] Moreover, near the close of his first narrative, he asks the reader, who is "likely to be turned over to Miss Clack," to do him "the favour of not believing a word she says, if she speaks of your humble servant" (210). Clack, for her part, seems even more scrupulous in trying to defend her moral conduct, developing her narrative into a kind of spiritual autobiography "of a Christian persecuted by the world" (295). One of the most interesting examples, however, of how narrative registers a character's anxieties about self-presentation is found in the final pages of Blake's second narrative, when Ablewhite's identity as the criminal is finally exposed.

The scene is a *tour de force* of narrative. Collins has already delayed the revelation of the thief by first introducing the surveillance of the bank as a future event for which we will have to wait, then sending all but Gooseberry after the wrong individuals, and finally postponing the lad's report of his investigations until the following morning. Which gradually brings us, after more delaying tactics—including the arrival of Cuff who, refusing to divulge immediately whom he suspects, seals the name in an envelope—to the door of room number ten of a public-house called "The Wheel of Fortune." Of course, several obstacles to the revelation of the *truth* remain: the door is locked, "some article of furniture [is] placed against it inside, as a barricade" (496), the face of the criminal is covered by both a pillow and a disguise, and (if that were not enough) the narrator of this segment, Blake, averts his eyes from the recognition scene. This reluctance to look, however, is significant not only as the last and most brilliant act of deferral in Collins's management of suspense, but also as a method by which Blake, the figurative writer, continues to construct his own innocence. Indeed, in turning us away from the deathbed and the impending recognition, the novel more powerfully exposes us to the ultimate aim of detection, which is to prove not who is guilty but who is innocent.

As a strategy, the narrative project of detection works to reassure: on the basis of just one crime, for which each individual in the society is potentially responsible, the chronicled investigation works toward repairing a community's reputation by declaring a specific party guilty and, following detection's deceptive logic, all others innocent.[10] But this self-interested purpose of marking the innocent is evident not only in the structure of the detective narrative (which moves to its conclusion in the designation of Ablewhite as guilty), but also in its mode of narration (which here dramatizes how Blake seeks to distinguish himself from the criminal). When Cuff "remove[s] the pillow," Blake witnesses what is uncovered:

> The man's swarthy face was placid and still; his black hair and beard were slightly, very slightly, discomposed. His eyes stared wide-open, glassy and vacant, at the ceiling. The filmy look and the fixed expression of them horrified me. I turned away, and went to the open window. The rest of them remained, where Sergeant Cuff remained, at the bed. (496)

In a scene remarkable for acts of looking and not looking, the emphasis on the horror inspired by the dead man's eyes is noteworthy. Blake apparently sees the eyes as a source of death and corruption—and he seems, in turning away, to recoil not so much from what he literally sees as from his own act of seeing. In walking away, he imposes a moral distance between himself and criminality, which is represented by the dead man and, potentially, by the uncontrolled looking of all the others. While Cuff is subject to a "strange fascination" and others are governed by a "strange curiosity" (497), Blake twice breaks away from the bed (496, 498), and returns only when he is "forced" (497) or commanded (498) to by the Sergeant. Whereas the others might seem morally callous, Blake's sensitivity is suggested by his "nerves [which] were not strong enough to bear it" (498). Whereas the others might seem to hunger for the removal of the disguise and the exposure of secrets, Blake tries to present a respectable restraint, an unwillingness to encroach upon another's private space.

Readers probably conceive of those others—against whom Blake defines himself—as possessing an enthusiasm not unlike their own and not unlike that of Gooseberry, whose excitement helps convey the sensational power of the scene. If the reactions of Gooseberry, whose "loose eyes rolled frightfully—not in terror, but in exultation" (497), bother us at all—and, at the very least, they disturb Blake—it is perhaps not because they seem highly unnatural but rather because they seem only too natural. Gooseberry's "high delight," "keener relish," and "breathless interest" (497–98) might remind readers of their own involuntary pleasure in a kind of subject matter that some Victorian critics would find reprehensible.[11] Certainly Blake views the scene as a place of moral danger, for he averts his own eyes, and now attempts to protect the boy: "There was something so hideous in the boy's enjoyment of the horror of the scene, that I took him by the two shoulders and put him out of the room" (497). Again, it is not the scene of the crime but the perception of it that unsettles Blake; it is the response that he finds "hideous"—"hideous," it appears, because Gooseberry's "enjoyment" seems to draw the boy into the very sordidness he looks upon, and because that "enjoyment" reflects a response to which Blake himself feels susceptible. Thus Blake's removal of the child (a common but here ironic symbol of innocence) figuratively suggests his continued attempt to preserve himself from contamination. But the boy returns, for he is, after all, "the irrepressible Gooseberry" (498), one apparently too young and natural to have learned repressive control over the self. Here such self-conscious behavior belongs to Blake, whose repression of his impulses reminds the reader that the scene is not only about exposing the doubleness of Ablewhite. For just as the detective narrative strips away a surface to disclose guilt, it also reveals a counteractivity—the building up of the repressive surface that will proclaim Blake's respectability.

Detection, *The Moonstone* implies, results in opposing activities: it peels away but covers over, scrutinizes but fails to see. Indeed, such contradiction underpins the detective enterprise where the very work of investigating (of probing social depths) conflicts with the project's ultimate aim of stopping investigation (of producing the solution that will allow society to reconstitute itself as innocent).[12] This commitment to closure characterizes the professional, who hopes to solve the current case quickly so as to move on to the next, and, even more so, the amateur like Blake, who, as a member of the suspect community, endures the period of detection as a necessary trial of the self. In the construction of a complete narrative pattern, the amateur finds a strategy of containing and repressing anxiety: the investigation and figurative writing are undertaken so that they might end; the unrest of narrative incompletion is tolerated only in the hope that it will soon dissipate. In other words, detection becomes a subtle method of social- and self-management, a repressive exercise in which a criminal—a scapegoat tactically burdened with society's guilt—is located and fenced round by narrative boundaries. Only in this way might the familiar and the proper return: the accustomed harmony, the appearance of innocence, and the comfortable obscurity once again might be enjoyed.

The reluctance to see that is evident in the repressive structure of the detective narrative also emerges in the day-to-day behavior of characters professing to respectability. Indeed, Blake's attempt to avoid the body of the criminal exemplifies the struggle for self-control faced by those who are simultaneously curious to uncover the secret and the scandalous, and troubled by the dangers implicit in such discoveries. After all, to view the hidden is to disrespect the very boundaries between public and private upon which their own repressive characters depend. Such contemplation taints the observers both by involving them in the underhanded and invasive practice of suspecting, probing, and interpreting others, and by imaginatively connecting them to the subjects of their investigations. In other words, to recognize and thus know the mean and ignoble is to betray their own innocence.

This consciousness of seeing as sin contributes not only to the distrust surrounding the detective efforts to recover the Moonstone, but also to the creation of the mystery of the diamond's loss. For Rachel shapes the development of the mystery by suppressing what she has seen, and she withholds her evidence because she feels disgraced by her act of observation. Admittedly, her shame is linked to Blake's actions in her sitting-room; but if her disgrace were limited only to *what* she sees, she would have a far easier time of exposing and repudiating Blake. In Rachel's consciousness, the episode in which Blake steals the diamond is reconfigured, becoming not so much an objective event as one in which she is actively involved. The nocturnal episode becomes a symbolic representation of desire: the virgin loses her jewel to the lover who secretly enters her room clad in a nightgown which, when later found, bears an incriminating stain.[13] While the novel does not, of course, suggest that Rachel reads the event in precisely that way, it does suggest that she possesses an unsettling intimation—however fuzzy and unarticulated—that the scene stages sexual desire and that she is a participant in that yearning. Indeed, her jewel is at risk of being stolen only because she has refused to let her mother " 'take charge of [her] Diamond' " (385); and she is awake to witness the theft only because, she later explains to Blake, " 'I was thinking of you' " (384). What troubles Rachel are feelings of her own complicity—that her preparation for the event and her passiveness during its unfolding signal her role as an accomplice in a forbidden act.

Thus the (apparent) crime of the theft of the diamond becomes psychologically linked with the metaphoric crime of illicit passion, so that Rachel becomes unable to condemn the former without also condemning the latter. One might also suggest that her very act of watching Blake's violation—as he stealthily invades her room and takes the Moonstone—becomes a reciprocal intrusion as she interpretively frames the scene—reading his guilt in his behavior (386-87)—and silently and secretly uncovers his hidden character. In either case, she is unable to remain aloof from the crime and the guilt; she uncovers not only Blake's disreputable self but also her own. Consequently, her feelings for Blake develop a new complexity, harboring as they do this distrust of both him and herself:

> "How can I make a *man* understand that a feeling which horrifies me at myself, can be a feeling that fascinates me at the same time? It's the breath of my life . . . and it's the poison that kills me—both in one!" (262)

Rejecting him—that is, exposing him as a criminal—would, figuratively, mean rejecting a crucial part of who she is. But to shelter what respectable society would view as a transgressive self, as she bravely does, means enduring inner turmoil. What she sees when she faces illicit desire in her sitting-room infects her with greater self-knowledge; but that discovery (which "fascinates" her and offers "the breath of [her] life") does not liberate her from society's oppressive judgment, which she has internalized and with which she punishes herself, feeling *horrified* and *poisoned*. Unlike those characters whose concern for their reputations would compel them to turn away from the crime and repudiate it, Rachel looks and maturely recognizes a kinship with what she sees. But though she admits her "'weakness'" (393) for what Blake the criminal represents—that, indeed, he exists within and that she "'can't tear [him] out of [her] heart'" (393)—her language of self-castigation reveals that she is unable to embrace this other side of the self. As she remarks, "'I despise myself even more heartily than I despise *him*!'" (393).

For Rachel, who refuses to look away, the act of outward observation cannot be divorced from inward observation and recognition—an anguished process of self-indictment from which she is rescued only by the surprising revelation that she, in fact, didn't see what she thought she saw.[14] But most characters concerned with their reputations are neither willing to endure Rachel's turmoil nor confident of gaining such a satisfying release from suffering. Consequently, they protect themselves by regulating what they see, for to view the hidden self (as it is represented, for example, by Blake's nocturnal actions or by Ablewhite's unmasking) is to encounter (and awaken) the repressed. Ezra Jennings, for example, is perceived as a moral danger, and his unpopularity extends even to "the pretty servant girl" who "received a modest little message from Ezra Jennings . . . with pursed-up lips, and with eyes which ostentatiously looked anywhere rather than look in his face" (409). With his dubious character and his conflicting appearance—he possesses "extraordinary parti-coloured hair" and "look[s] old and young both together" (408)—Jennings seems to become a visual reminder of the complexities and contradictions of the self that most individuals wish to suppress.

Similarly, Colonel Herncastle

> found himself avoided by everybody. . . . The mystery of the Colonel's life got in the Colonel's way, and outlawed him, as you may say, among his own people. The men wouldn't let him into

> their clubs; the women—more than one—whom he wanted to marry, refused him; friends and relations got too near-sighted to see him in the street. (33-34)

When Herncastle calls once at the Verinder home to wish Rachel a happy birthday, Lady Verinder tells Betteredge to return the message " 'that Miss Verinder is engaged, and that *I* decline to see him' " (35). What we have here is a concerted effort of social and personal control where the very refusal to "see" Herncastle—a decision which, ironically, depends on an act of seeing, of recognition—expresses the repressive desire that he cease to exist. Society polices itself by excluding Herncastle, a measure that works simultaneously to excise his corrupting presence and to warn its members not to follow his example.[15] But the threat of rebellion remains: for although both society and the individual repress the outlaw—forcing him to live "a solitary, vicious, underground life" (34)—he will eventually return. Indeed, the drama of *The Moonstone* inheres in the havoc of that return (as Herncastle wreaks his revenge on the society that excluded him) and in the desperate detective and narrative efforts to impose order on the resulting confusion. Thus, in a sense, the work unfolds as a psychological drama where the purpose of explanation is to isolate and subdue the outlaw, and thereby recover one's respectable identity. Storytelling becomes an attempt to stuff the genie back in the bottle—to create a repressive structure to contain the forces of misrule. Such a framework might seem reassuringly in place by the end of the narrative project, particularly when Murthwaite, in the last of the book's documents, reports seeing "the Moonstone look[ing] forth once more, over the walls of the sacred city in which its story first began" (521). But as the novel's last sentences remind us, the circle images not completion but cyclic recurrence, and thus a power at odds with the narrative intention to enclose and control: "So the years pass, and repeat each other; so the same events revolve in the cycles of time. What will be the next adventures of the Moonstone? Who can tell?" (522). Although Murthwaite's letter is employed by Blake and Bruff as part of their repressive narrative strategy, it resists that function; it raises in its final words questions that subvert closure, questions that, in fact, posit the very existence of the transgressive energy which is destined to break free again from its confinement.

To mention tactics of social- and self-regulation is not to deride or dismiss them, for some kind of discipline and order seem necessary to the well-being of the community. Yet to consider these tactics is, at least, to acknowledge what many of the novel's characters seem reluctant to admit—namely, the complexity of a self that needs to be regulated. Admittedly, the very attempt to conceal a disreputable self implies an unsettling intimation of that self, but most characters wish to see no more, even turning away from the conventional detective act of discovering others' guilt in the desperate attempt to confirm their own innocence. After all, in *The Moonstone* detection is not an activity for respectable individuals who, if they can, pass on its sordid duties to paid professionals like Cuff and Seegrave. Even more convenient is the work of the Brahmins whose tracking down and punishing of Ablewhite seems to preserve, for example, the innocence of Blake, who thereby remains free from such contaminating activity. We may smile at Betteredge's reports of his repeated attacks of "detective-fever," but within the world of the novel the lure of investigation truly seems a "disease" (135) and an "infection" (207), an insidious threat to the individual's moral health. Although excited by the prospect of probing mystery and uncovering secrets, Betteredge strains against the temptation, recognizing that investigation threatens not only the investigated (for example, Rachel and Rosanna, whom he honorably attempts to screen) but also the investigator, whose self-control and self-respect are jeopardized. Consequently, Betteredge hotly contradicts Cuff's suggestion that he has been adopted as the

Sergeant's assistant, swearing to Lady Verinder "'that I never, to my knowledge, helped this abominable detective business, in any way, from first to last'" (187). As an immoral business, detection involves its participants not only in unworthy suspicions but also in dishonesty; in pursuit of the *truth* the detective can fabricate lies, and in pursuit of the duplicitous criminal he too can appear to be someone he is not.

If the ultimate intention of detection is the proving of innocence, then the refusal to detect paradoxically becomes part of that project. Refraining from investigation means preserving the self from contamination and disintegration, because, as Cuff's interview with Mrs. Yolland suggests, the deceptive practice of detection destabilizes the detective's identity. For Betteredge, watching Cuff and Mrs. Yolland is like watching "a stage play," an analogy that underlines Cuff's performance as he proceeds in his "usual roundabout manner" and "dismal underground way" (139) to obtain information about Rosanna. Who is the Cuff who can so easily assume a new part, or, for that matter, who is the Betteredge who has accompanied the Sergeant on this mission of trickery? Betteredge records his anxiety:

> I began to question whether my share in the proceedings was quite as harmless a one as I had thought it. It might be all in the way of the Sergeant's business to mystify an honest woman by wrapping her round in a network of lies; but it was my duty to have remembered, as a good Protestant, that the father of lies is the Devil—and that mischief and the Devil are never far apart. (140)

Here Betteredge tries to distinguish himself from the dissembling detective, citing his "duty . . . as a good Protestant" as if to reconfirm the solidity and respectability of his identity. Betteredge fears dishonesty because such shifting and duplicitous behavior undermines his ability to believe in a stable self.[16] What Collins builds in this scene, then, are two connected dramas; as in the episode of

Ablewhite's unmasking, the suspenseful process of detection and revelation merges with the moral adventure of the viewer who struggles to disassociate himself from the *crime* of the investigation. For readers the pleasure of the scene is similarly complex as we enjoy the anticipation of Cuff's discoveries, and the uncertainty and, of course, humor generated by Betteredge's repeated efforts to leave the cottage and thus distance himself from Cuff's detection. Perhaps we even enjoy the excitement of feeling that for us, as for Betteredge, watching means danger.

While the novel's page-turning readers (who must necessarily identify with the *sordid* investigations of Cuff and Gooseberry) seem pushed toward recognizing the complexities of the self, many of the novel's characters attempt to avoid such self-recognition, clinging instead to a notion of a unified, respectable self. Such a character is Mr. Bruff who, on a stake-out at the bank, shrinks from the prospect of tailing his suspect. Unable to delegate the work to either Gooseberry or his "second man" (483) who has disappeared, Bruff asks Blake, "'What is to be done? . . . *We* can't degrade ourselves by following him'" (483). For Bruff, detection—that is, engaging in surreptitious activity oneself and imagining such behavior from another—contravenes the code of respectability whereby surface appearance identifies the individual. Despite his reservations, Bruff, along with Blake, follows the suspect, whom he discovers to be the wrong man. Yet that failure to succeed as a detective comforts Bruff, suggesting his innate respectability and thus his inability to be different from himself. "'It's greatly to our credit,'" the lawyer explains to Blake, that "'you and I are the two worst amateur detectives that ever tried their hands at the trade'" (484). Of course, the very need to interpret himself in this way implies Bruff's anxiety about the precariousness of his identity, a concern voiced earlier when he enjoins Blake to silence on the subject of their detection: "'For Heaven's sake don't mention it. I should be ruined if it was known'" (483).

Bruff fears the erosion of his self-image and, consequently, finds consolation in an unsuccessful detective foray that quickly returns him to the respectable world of surface identity and public credentials in which he likes to believe. For his detective journey concludes at his own chemist, and the suspicious "'man in the grey suit [proves to have] been thirty years in the chemist's service'" (484). Similarly, the investigation conducted by Bruff's "second man" seems to disprove the notion of doubleness and thus to confirm the credibility of the lawyer's world, as his suspect "'turns out . . . to be a most respectable master ironmonger in Eastcheap'" (484).

Just as the Brahmins' attempt to keep a constant watch upon the diamond becomes a figurative realization of fears about surveillance, so the impact of that detection on the Brahmins themselves signifies that loss of identity which Betteredge and Bruff fear. When Murthwaite first encounters the three Brahmins on the evening of Rachel's birthday, he is puzzled, remarking that there "'is a mystery about their conduct that I can't explain. They have doubly sacrificed their caste—first, in crossing the sea; secondly, in disguising themselves as jugglers'" (79). The explanation for this behavior, we discover, is that they have undertaken the underground work of detection, which supposedly so alienates them from their class identity that each, at the book's end, is cast out to wander until death on a pilgrimage of purification (521). In *The Moonstone* detection foregrounds self-division, a contradiction which emerges less somberly in the portrait of Sergeant Cuff, whose passion for roses (Betteredge informs the Sergeant) "'seems an odd taste . . . for a man in your line of life'" (108). But this complexity is, obviously, not just the problem of the detective; it is a typically human condition, as Cuff suggests when he informs Betteredge "'that the nature of a man's tastes is, most times, as opposite as possible to the nature of a man's business'" (108). With the sharp division between his professional life and his private life, symbolized by his retirement cottage at Dorking, Cuff is reminiscent of Dickens's Wemmick, whose professional life with Jaggers alternates with his private life in his "castle" at Walworth.[17] The public/private opposition appears most emphatically, of course, in Godfrey Ablewhite, whose life similarly divides between his public role, represented by the charitable gentleman, and the symbolically private life of the hidden sanctuary, represented by the "villa in the suburbs which was not taken in his own name" (503).

While Cuff seems remarkably comfortable with his ability to inhabit both a public and private identity,[18] most characters fear such division and contradiction. Perhaps it is because Cuff, like Wemmick, must frequent the world of the criminal in his professional life that he gladly escapes to a private life where he may cultivate very different experiences and values. More commonly, however, characters face just the opposite problem: because they project innocence publicly, their private lives can represent only a falling off, a discrepancy which, because it must be hidden, becomes analogous to the criminal self that Ablewhite conceals. Just as the conventional detective attempts to separate innocence from guilt in society, so these individuals attempt to enforce such a division within themselves by repressing or disowning the transgressive self. Indeed, as we have seen, the very effort to refrain from detection becomes a kind of detection, of self-policing in which a character would regulate his curiosity, confirm his respectability, suppress the recognition that would discern something of himself in the duplicity of the criminal.

It should not be surprising that the detective novel concerns itself with both external and internal acts of policing. When characters are externally judged according to the simple oppositions of good and evil, innocence and guilt, they will probably attend to those same artificial categories in monitoring their behavior and in presenting themselves to the world. In *The Moonstone,* as in *Caleb*

Williams and *Bleak House,* external surveillance compels internal surveillance, and thus the need to hide the *criminal* self. While the autobiographical impulse of Caleb, Esther, and Blake, for example, apparently represents self-expression, their figurative texts expose how self-presentation may function as self-censorship. Caleb attempts to construct his innocence by denying his culpability; Esther strives for legitimacy precisely by being self-less (that is, by erasing her tainted self), and Blake seeks to advertise his respectability by suppressing his guilt and contradictions. In his narration Blake tries, for example, to correct Betteredge's earlier portrayal of him, protesting against the steward's claim that his "foreign training" has left him "with so many different sides to his character, all more or less jarring with each other, that he seemed to pass his life in a state of perpetual contradiction with himself" (47). According to Blake, Betteredge

> has, in his own quaint way, interpreted seriously one of his young mistress's many satirical references to my foreign education; and has persuaded himself that he actually saw those French, German, and Italian sides to my character, which my lively cousin only professed to discover in jest, and which never had any real existence, except in our good Betteredge's own brain. (324)

Probably we accept part of this argument, recognizing that Betteredge's "picture" (324) of Blake's character is necessarily shaped by the character—the "quaint way"—of the author who produced it. Yet the same reservations attend our judgment of Blake's self-presentation, which may be seen as the product of his desire to appear as a stable, consistent, and innocent character. In his attempt to establish his respectability, Blake would cover over the "many different sides to his character"; he would deny the complexity and depths of the self suggested, for instance, by his removal of the diamond, his anxiety about his guilt, and his period of "foreign training." In contemplating the latter, we consider not only the effects of education in unfixing and thus complicating his character, but also the largely secret but possibly disturbing facts of that past existence.

Blake's life in "foreign parts" (62) becomes a sign of that otherness, which he cannot escape when he returns to England. In a sense, geography and time are employed to delineate Blake, to distinguish between his surface character (represented by England and his pose in the present of the adventure as Rachel's honorable suitor) and the depth it hides (represented by the Continent, the past, and the dishonor and selfishness of his accumulating debts). Furthermore, in Betteredge's report early in his narrative that a "strange gentleman, speaking English with a foreign accent, came . . . to see Mr. Franklin Blake on business" (62), we may sense the surfacing of this suppressed otherness. Betteredge even suggests a metaphoric identification between the foreigner and Blake's disreputable side when he records his suspicion that "some imprudence of Mr. Franklin's on the Continent . . . had followed him to England" (62). Of course, Blake will later explain the incident in his own narrative, where he attempts to accomplish psychologically (by proclaiming his innocence) what Lady Verinder accomplishes literally (by paying the debt): he attempts to turn the intrusive foreigner away. Blake tries to link himself to "thousands of other honest men" who have been unable to repay a loan on time, but as his account continues we, in fact, recognize his dishonesty and unwillingness to accept responsibility for his actions: "I sent the man a bill. My name was unfortunately too well known on such documents: he failed to negotiate it" (375). While Blake's use of "unfortunately" suggests his desire to portray himself as an unlucky victim, the other details of the sentence actually implicate him in a repeated and thus consciously dishonest practice of passing out worthless "documents." Indeed, his narrative explanation of the incident, in which he is dishonest to both the reader and himself, becomes a version of his financial transactions, a text which, like the name appended to it, cannot be trusted.

The desire for self-control pervades the novel, from Blake's efforts to prove his innocence, to Betteredge's attempts to avoid detecting, to Clack's self-approving descriptions of how she gets "the better of [her] fallen nature" (248). While Clack's pose is the most transparent, her writing usefully foregrounds the subject of self-vigilance: she depicts the world in terms of spiritual conflict, with our "evil passions" waiting to "pounce on us unawares" (222), and with our primary defense existing in our self-awareness of that threat. A similar emphasis on the control exerted by self-consciousness underpins Jennings's remarks to Blake on the effects of opium:

> "Under the stimulating influence, the latest and most vivid impressions left on your mind—namely, the impressions relating to the Diamond—would be likely, in your morbidly sensitive nervous condition, to become intensified in your brain, and would subordinate to themselves your judgment and your will—exactly as an ordinary dream subordinates to itself your judgment and your will." (435)

The implication here is that self-control operates as part of consciousness itself, which through the policing power of the "judgment" and the "will" attempts to repress the discordant and thus provide the semblance of order. In Jennings's commentary, the self emerges as a conflicted entity, whose fragile balance and composure can be overturned merely by the ingestion of a drug or the onset of dreams.

Obviously, some degree of self-control is necessary to the smooth functioning of both individual and society, but too much regulation—too much self-censorship and denial—creates its own problems. Perhaps no character in *The Moonstone* more powerfully illustrates the dangers of self-policing than Rosanna Spearman. As she explains in her letter to Blake, " 'My life was not a very hard life to bear, while I was a thief. It was only when they had taught me at the reformatory to feel my own degradation, and to try for better things, that the days grew long and weary' " (350). The reformatory attempts "to save forlorn women from drifting back into bad ways, after they had got released from prison" (22) by implanting the controlling function of the law within the women themselves. As long as Spearman is unconscious of her guilt, she remains content; but her education in the reformatory makes her degraded, instilling a judgmental self-consciousness, splitting her apart so that she must look down upon her lower self, a self that is thus monitored even after it is "released from prison." But though she is now taught to recognize her criminality, she is unable to recognize and thus believe in a legitimate self: " 'I felt the dreadful reproach that honest people—even the kindest of honest people—were to me in themselves. A heart-breaking sensation of loneliness kept with me, go where I might, and do what I might, and see what persons I might' " (350). In a desperate attempt to escape her isolation, she pursues a romance with Blake, but his apparent failure even to notice her only confirms her suspicions that she is unworthy—that, indeed, she is nothing but a degraded woman. And that, of course, is the woman she has been taught to repudiate. It is perhaps not surprising, then, that her final gesture is her suicidal plunge beneath the surface of the quicksand, an act in which she follows the logic of self-policing to its horrifying conclusion and suppresses herself completely.

At the end of *Caleb Williams* the oppressive narrative structure that the hero develops to defend his innocence is emphatically broken: Caleb simultaneously confesses his culpability and repudiates his autobiographical project. But in *The Moonstone* there is no such abandonment of the narrative enterprise. Here writing similarly proceeds as an affirming of innocence, although Blake, for example, does not eventually admit the repressive strategy of his storytelling. Indeed, in *The Moonstone,* where most of the figurative writing occurs after the mystery has been *solved,* the narrative pretends to unfold as the comfortable recording of retrospective knowledge rather than as the discovery of what is disturbingly new. We do read of Blake's dramatic recognition of his nightgown and his guilt, but that moment is included only so that it may be denied by subsequent scenes that prove his blamelessness. Writing in *The Moonstone* becomes largely a method of self-performance and control, a tactic that is not significantly challenged by any character, with the possible exception of Ezra Jennings. Certainly, Jennings seems to resist the self-interested motivations of storytelling by refusing to fashion his self-image: he " 'scorn[s] the guilty evasion of living under an assumed name' " (421); he doesn't " 'profess . . . to tell [his] story . . . to any man' " (419); on his deathbed, he leaves instructions that his papers be placed with him in his coffin (511–12). Yet this character, whose own "story is a blank" (511), becomes a major participant in the construction of Blake's public identity. What we find in *The Moonstone*'s account of an investigation is ultimately an avoidance of investigation—a discovery that, in effect, positions us in the role of challenging the narrative's power, of being the novel's true detectives. In *The Moonstone* the reader detects—not merely mimicking or anticipating the discoveries that free Blake and incriminate Ablewhite, but closely inspecting the very account of the solution and finding in it a case worth investigating. The brilliance of *The Moonstone* lies not only in the superb craftsmanship with which it plots an investigation, but also in the skill with which it simultaneously casts suspicion on that inquiry, inviting its readers to scrutinize the narrative records of the case, to deduce what has been suppressed, and to stir up those mysteries which its own characters have been reluctant to see.

FIVE

A "Paralysing Spectacle"

Authority and Submission in *The Hound of the Baskervilles*

In the second chapter of Arthur Conan Doyle's *The Hound of the Baskervilles* (1902), Dr. Mortimer reads to Holmes and Watson a narrative explaining "'the coming of the hound which is said to have plagued the family so sorely ever since'" (14).[1] This account of the origin of the curse begins by describing how Hugo Baskerville and his companions kidnap a maiden, how she escapes by climbing down the ivy that covers the south wall of Baskerville Hall, and how Hugo and his hounds pursue her as she flees homeward over the moor. In its unfolding, however, the story undergoes a sudden ironic reversal whereby the supposed hunter becomes the hunted; like Actaeon who is torn apart by his own hounds, Hugo is chased down and destroyed by "'a great, black beast, shaped like a hound, yet larger than any hound that ever mortal eye has rested upon'" (13). In the introduction to this tale, the anonymous descendant of Hugo tries to impose significant structure and thus meaning upon the succession of incidents by interpreting the beast and its actions as the work of divine " 'Justice,' " as a poetically just punishment in which " 'foul passions' " (seemingly embodied by the retributive hound) are " 'loosed to our undoing' " (11). This pattern of reversal repeats itself in the investigative narrative that Watson relates: here the criminal Stapleton, Hugo's descendant who, according to Holmes, inherits his ancestor's " 'physical and spiritual' " (139) characteristics, likewise seems to be defeated by the evil passions he is unable to control. Indeed, Stapleton's potential as a victim is implicit in Watson's first encounter with the naturalist, who excuses himself in mid-conversation to pursue a "small fly or moth": in his "grey clothes and jerky, zigzag, irregular progress," the collector of butterflies and moths appears "not unlike some huge moth himself" (69). It is Holmes, of course, who now performs the work of justice, hunting down the hunter so that, as the detective predicts to Watson, " 'he will be fluttering in our net as helpless as one of his own butterflies. A pin, a cork, and a card, and we add him to the Baker Street collection!' " (140).

In the manuscript of 1742 that Mortimer reads, the narrator tries to control the terror and wildness of events by affirming the presence of a divinity that has shaped the story into a meaningful pattern of sin and appropriate punishment. In the secular, late-Victorian narrative of Watson, Holmes's authority derives partly from his assumption of the role of absent providence: through his superior intelligence he contrives the pattern of poetic justice, transforming bewildering mystery (which camouflages the criminal's actions) into an artful design that expresses the detective's mastery. Through narrative devices such as its repeated images of nets (representing the authorial plots or schemes of both the hunter Stapleton and the hunter Holmes), the novel delineates an adventure that is simultaneously a pursuit of prey and a pursuit of significant design. For Holmes, perceiving the hunter's net means isolating "power and design" (38) from the confusion of mystery; it means discerning both the criminal and his motives. For the reader, perceiving Holmes's net means witnessing the skill with which the detective absorbs Stapleton's scheme into his own controlling narrative.

This competition for storytelling supremacy is a recurring ingredient in early detective fiction. Much of the dramatic interest in *Caleb Williams* centers upon the conflict between Caleb and Falkland as each tries to contain the other within an imprisoning narrative. The Dupin stories also portray struggles for narrative power as Poe's brilliant analyst pits himself against rival detectives and criminals; the culmination of these contests is, of course, Dupin's victory over Minister D—, whose designs are absorbed into the more cunning and encompassing scheme of the detective. In Collins's *The Woman in White* the investigations of Hartright and Marian proceed as a method of uncovering the conspiracy engineered by Fosco and Glyde and thus attaining power over both that plot and its authors. Here, in *The Hound of the Baskervilles,* Holmes describes a similar project of capturing his opponent, informing Watson, " 'My nets are closing upon him, even as his are upon Sir Henry' " (127). Holmes triumphs by assuming an authorial position outside the criminal plot where he can direct the action and implement that final ironic twist of the narrative that indicates closure. That his " 'case becomes rounded off' "(145) and that the detective can now stand outside it seem further emphasized both by the speed with which Holmes moves on to investigate other "affairs" (158) and by his provision of "A Retrospection," a summation in which his authorial voice dominates the concluding pages, demonstrating the ability "'to put into a single connected narrative one of the most singular and sensational crimes of modern times'" (145).

Yet, as we have seen, early detective fiction not only displays the storytelling prowess of the detective but also skeptically queries his motives and accomplishments, and *The Hound of the Baskervilles* is no exception. Even as Doyle's novel provides these signs of Holmes's narrative authority, it also raises questions about the legitimacy and extent of that authority.[2] For example, is this detective securely established as a character posed in opposition to the criminal? Or is he subject—if not to a complete reversal like Hugo and Stapleton—to, at least, significant contradiction and complexity? Can Holmes legitimately stand outside the world upon which he authorially imposes justice and order? Or is the detective also implicated in the failings of that world? Indeed, is the "case" over which he presides so simple that it can be understood and thereby possessed in the form of a tidy explanatory narrative with a clearly defined beginning, middle, and end?

We can begin reflecting on these issues by exploring some of the connections that seem to link Holmes, like Dupin before him, to the very criminality he pursues. A particularly resonant moment in the characterization of the detective occurs in Watson's second report when, in venturing out upon the moor at night with Sir Henry in search of the convict, he experiences an unexpected vision of another man standing upon "the jagged pinnacle of a granite tor" (98). This other man, who we later learn is Holmes, "stood with his legs a little separated, his arms folded, his head bowed, as if he were brooding over that enormous wilderness of peat and granite which lay behind him. He might have been the very spirit of that terrible place" (98). Certainly, in one sense, the passage strengthens our positive impression of Holmes as a lonely hero who must endure the trials of the wilderness in his battle against evil. Furthermore, the figure's elevated and pensive stance upon the tor suggests the way Holmes functions for his age as a surrogate creator of order; like the engendering "Spirit" in *Paradise Lost* which "with mighty wings outspread, / Dovelike sat'st brooding on the vast abyss" (I.20–21),[3] Holmes seems to be "brooding over that enormous wilderness of peat and granite" in his authorial effort to transform the hostile chaos of mystery into a meaningful design. But in concluding that the man "might have been the very spirit of that terrible place," Watson introduces ambiguity, suggesting not so much Holmes's superiority to his environment as the possibility that he embodies its essence. Later, when Watson locates this mysterious figure's hut and waits inside, he sustains the opposition, wondering, "Was he our malignant enemy, or was he by chance our guardian angel?" (121). Holmes's entrance shortly thereafter seems to resolve this uncertainty, at least for Watson, from whom "a crushing weight of responsibility seemed in an instant to be lifted" (122).

Yet is Holmes's role as "the man on the tor" only a technical device of mystery, providing the readerly satisfactions of temporary puzzlement, suspense, and surprise? Or does Holmes's ambiguous position as the "secret man" (121) represent the very complexities and contradictions of a character who, at times, seems intriguingly similar to the hunter he hunts down? For example, Watson's description of the "dry glitter in [Stapleton's] eyes" (77) echoes the "hard, dry glitter which shot from [Holmes's eyes] when he was keenly interested" (20). Similarly, when Stapleton begins his explanation for living on the moor by remarking to the narrator, " 'Queer spot to choose, is it not?'. . . as if in answer to my thought" (71), we recall Holmes's deductive abilities; Stapleton, like the detective, even accounts for his surprising inference, referring Watson to " 'your expression as you surveyed the moor out of our window' " (72). But perhaps the most remarkable conjunction of detective and criminal occurs when Holmes attempts to trace the man in the hansom cab. Although the spy has eluded him in Regent Street, Holmes notes the cab number, which in turn leads to the driver whom he proceeds to question. Holmes learns that, on leaving the cab, the bearded man "mentioned his name," a revelation that causes the detective to "cast a swift glance of triumph" at Watson, before remarking, "'That was imprudent. What was the name that he mentioned?'" The cabman replies, "'His name . . . was Mr Sherlock Holmes'" (49). Obviously this scene is vastly different from the tragic recognition of Oedipus or the distressing discovery of Collins's Franklin Blake (who seems to detect himself as the thief of the Moonstone); here the supposed moment of revelation is a mere trick, a surprise concocted by Holmes's opponent. Yet it is as a skillful contrivance that the moment works to link Holmes with the criminal, whom he now describes as "'a foeman . . . worthy of our steel'" (51). In constructing the scene so that the detective is detected, his expectation of "triumph" dramatically undercut, the criminal displays a narrative artistry that anticipates Holmes's crafting of ironic reversal in hunting down the hunter and closing his case. As Holmes acknowledges, "'He knew our number, knew that Sir Henry Baskerville had consulted me, spotted who I was in Regent Street, conjectured that I had got the number of the cab and would lay my hands on the driver, and so sent back this audacious message'" (51). The "message" by which he shocks Holmes is the criminal's expression of power, a demonstration that he has so clearly foreseen the detective's moves that he has successfully accommodated them to his own plan of action.

At the conclusion of this first encounter with the criminal, Holmes admits, "'I've been checkmated in London'" (51). This familiar analogy between the work of the detective and the playing of a game blurs the moral distance between the two opponents. Indeed, to play the game well the detective must repress his own emotional involvement and respond with cool reason to an adversary who, after all, is necessary for the detective's (and reader's) pleasure. In *The Hound of the Baskervilles* the gap between the detective and the criminal is even narrower because both seek power in essentially the same way: by creating moments that shock a particular audience. Although the detective's construction of startling effects may suggest egoism and an insensitivity to the nervous plight of his chosen audience, Holmes is not unusual in displaying this ability to surprise. Dickens's Bucket, for example, exhibits fine narrative instincts and a rather callous disregard for Sir Leicester Dedlock's nerves when he stages the astonishing entrance of the criminal Hortense. Similarly, Poe's Dupin contrives a sensational scene for both the Prefect and the narrator when he miraculously produces the purloined letter. What is unusual is that in Doyle's novel the crimes themselves are also assaults on victims' nervous systems. Stapleton's victims—Charles, Selden, and Henry—suffer not from physical contact with the hound but from the overpowering horror produced by its sudden approach. Through an artful application of phosphorus, Stapleton transforms the dog into a monstrous creature that has the effect of scaring Sir Charles and Selden literally to their deaths; as Holmes remarks, " 'the one frightened to death by the very sight of a beast which he thought to be supernatural, the other driven to his end in his wild flight to escape from it' " (130). As for the third victim, Sir Henry, whose encounter with the hound forms the novel's climax, "the shock of the night's adventures had shattered his nerves, and before morning he lay delirious in a high fever, under the care of Dr Mortimer. The two of them were destined to travel together round the world before Sir Henry had become once more the hale, hearty man that he had been before he became master of that ill-omened estate" (155).

In depicting how Stapleton uses shock as a criminal weapon, the novel indirectly critiques Holmes's strategies of surprise and even Watson's techniques of suspense and sudden revelation. As it is fashioned by Stapleton, Holmes, and Watson, plot enforces an unequal relationship between the control of the knowing artist and the vulnerability of the unknowing participant who is manipulated, fooled, and astonished. Yet preceding all these narrative efforts is the strange legend of "the Hound of the Baskervilles" itself, which functions in the novel much like an allegory of narrative's power to upset and subdue. As the first sentence of that narrative suggests, the passing down of the story through the generations of the family suggestively becomes the transmission of the curse itself: " 'Of the origin of the Hound of the Baskervilles there have been many statements, yet as I come in a direct line from Hugo Baskerville, and as I had the story from my father, who also had it from his, I have set it down with all belief that it occurred even as is here set forth' " (11). That there are "many" versions, including the preferred "story" that follows, emphasizes the inaccessibility of the original moment; what exists instead are linguistic reproductions of the absent event, narratives which hound succeeding generations by re-presenting the beast and its terrifying effects.

The legend thus functions as a curse by preserving for its readers and listeners the nervous trauma that supposedly characterizes the *original* scene of suffering. The story of Hugo, the maid, and the hound (11–14) proceeds as a descent into nervous and mental derangement, as a chronicling of the ravages of shock and fear. We read that the kidnapped maiden " 'upstairs was like to have her wits turned at the singing and shouting and terrible oaths which came up to her from below,' " and " 'in the stress of her fear' " she escapes. Discovering her flight, Hugo becomes " 'as one that hath a devil' " and pursues her with his hounds. When " 'some sense came back to their crazed minds,' " his thirteen companions follow him, encountering first a shepherd " 'so crazed with fear that he could scarce speak,' " and then the unnerving sight of Hugo's riderless black mare, which causes them to ride " 'close together, for a great fear was on them.' " Rapidly the account unfolds, registering the effects of the horrifying experience on the hounds who " 'were whimpering in a cluster . . . some slinking away and some, with starting hackles and staring eyes, gazing down the narrow valley before them' "; on the " 'unhappy maid' " who " 'had fallen, dead of fear and of fatigue' "; and, finally, on the companions who boldly venture down into the valley to witness the beast tearing " 'the throat out of Hugo Baskerville' " and turning " 'its blazing eyes and dripping jaws upon them. . . . One, it is said, died that very night of what he had seen, and the other twain were but broken men for the rest of their days.' "

Without the narratives that recount and thus imaginatively repeat these events, the force of the original shocks would soon dissipate. But thanks to the manuscript, for example, that debilitating power is still active, having most recently afflicted Sir Charles, whose " 'nervous system,' " Mortimer reports, " 'was strained to breaking point. He had taken this legend which I have read you exceedingly to heart . . . ' " (18). Like a virus, the energy of that original moment of nervous excess is transmitted outward, infecting Charles and later other victims—Henry, Watson, even the reader. For so much of what is exciting in the novel results figuratively from the deliberate restaging of the initial shocking event. The manuscript reproduces the incident for Charles; Stapleton, learning " 'about the family hound' " from Charles and knowing " 'that a shock would kill him' " (160), recreates the chase scene; Holmes, in his desire to round off his case, cooperates in staging the hounding of Sir Henry; and Watson, in penning his account, reconstructs the stressful adventure for his readers. Thus the enervating shocks are disseminated, and Holmes and Watson—supposedly the agents of order—are implicated in the process of transmission.

Holmes is, of course, successful in identifying criminal motivation, in defeating Stapleton, and in preserving Henry's life. Indeed, one could argue that in detecting human agency behind apparently supernatural effects and in offering his explanatory solution, Holmes actually eradicates the anxieties that mystery produces. Yet before Holmes imposes the figurative closure that will supposedly free the case's participants from the suspense of narrative incompletion, he himself contributes to the nervous unrest that he should be alleviating. Watson cautiously addresses this failing in the great detective at the beginning of the novel's climactic chapter:

> One of Sherlock Holmes's defects—if, indeed, one may call it a defect—was that he was exceedingly loth to communicate his full plans to any other person until the instant of their fulfilment. Partly it came no doubt from his own masterful nature, which loved to dominate and surprise those who were around him. Partly also from his professional caution, which urged him never to take any chances. The result, however, was very trying for those who were acting as his agents and assistants. I had often suffered under it, but never more so than during that long drive in the darkness. (146)

In secretly developing his "plans," Holmes seeks to exercise his authorial power over not only the enemy, whom he hopes to catch off guard, but also his own "agents and assistants," whom he loves to "surprise" and thus "dominate." By explaining Holmes's desire to astonish in terms of this love of domination, Watson allows us to consider how the "masterful" Holmes, like Stapleton, functions as an oppressive figure of authority. While Holmes is certainly not as malicious nor as dangerous as Stapleton, he similarly employs the narrative strategy of surprise to create a gap between the strength of his prescience and composure and the vulnerability of his startled subjects. Here, as they "drive in the darkness" toward the encounter with the hound itself, Watson suffers the trials of suspense as he awaits the unknown, the startling experience that Holmes, throughout their relationship, constantly provides. The surprise may be one of those initially unaccountable deductions with which Holmes so often bewilders Watson: "'You have been at your club all day, I perceive,'" Holmes pronounces, causing Watson's exclamation, "'My dear Holmes!'" (26). Or the display of power may be more theatrically astounding, as when Holmes fashions the stunning climax to Watson's hunt for "the man on the tor" in chapter 11. Functioning as the surrogate for the detective in Holmes's supposed absence, Watson attempts to orchestrate his own moment of surprise and revelation, setting his trap and waiting nervously inside the hut as the mysterious man approaches.

But Holmes, the actual man on the tor, manages to transform the encounter into a demonstration of his own foresight and control, uttering words that so unexpectedly shift the direction of the scene and puncture its tension: " 'It is a lovely evening, my dear Watson. . . . I really think that you will be more comfortable outside than in' " (122).

That Holmes "loved to dominate and surprise" is evident from both of these examples, which emphasize the detective's pleasure in startling Watson and thus reading his own power as it is registered on the doctor's nervous system. Watson reports in the first instance that Holmes "laughed at my bewildered expression" (26), and in the second that "his grey eyes danc[ed] with amusement as they fell upon my astonished features" (122). This hint of sadism is perhaps more strongly reflected in the enjoyment Holmes derives from surprising and subduing Stapleton; as he envisions catching the hunter in his act of hunting, Holmes "burst into one of his rare fits of laughter," a response that "always boded ill to somebody" (140). In crafting moments of astonishment and, indeed, in fashioning his case upon the same principles of surprise, Holmes commits himself to an artistic practice in which his own pleasure depends upon the discomfort of others. For the investigating Holmes desires not just a victory over the rival plotter. He desires to create a triumph of such stunning effect that it impresses itself on both the criminal whose astonishment testifies to his being outwitted, and on his own audience (of Lestrade, Henry, Watson, and even Watson's readers) whose nervous trials become evidence of the detective's inventive genius.

This darker side of Holmes's method is evident from the very beginning of his investigation, when he shows Watson the Ordnance map he has been studying and remarks: " 'This, then, is the stage upon which tragedy has been played, and upon which we may help to play it again' " (27). These are disconcerting words because they seem to dissolve the opposition between detective and criminal, suggesting their possible cooperation in recreating "tragedy." Here we sense the degree to which Holmes's plotting replicates the criminal's, and how the detective is thus implicated in producing an analogous suffering. The reader, however, is likely to avoid an interpretation that would blame Holmes; after all, investigation is necessarily an act of repetition as the authorial detective pieces together and thus writes the illegible story of the crime. Furthermore, here is a case in which, as Holmes explains in "A Retrospection," "'a complete knowledge of the whole business'" (165) is not sufficient. Proof is needed: "'There seemed to be no alternative but to catch him red-handed, and to do so we had to use Sir Henry, alone and apparently unprotected, as a bait'" (166). Therefore Holmes must "help to play" the tragedy again, a dramatic undertaking which recalls Ezra Jennings's experiment in *The Moonstone*, where he re-stages the theft of the diamond for an audience of Betteredge, Bruff, and Rachel. Yet Holmes's production is not a harmless, intellectual activity cut off from the criminal world it hopes to illuminate; here the theatrical metaphors—stage, tragedy, play—link Holmes's project to Stapleton's as he similarly manages a drama of shocking impact. In *The Hound of the Baskervilles* to repeat is to reshock, and Holmes's repetition proceeds partly from his own artistic pride, his desire "'to have [his] case well rounded and complete'" (129). While Holmes obviously intends to control the dramatic horror by preventing the hound from catching Henry, he nevertheless participates in producing a sensational scene, another nerve-racking plot which reproduces and thus perpetuates the original suffering.

Holmes admits that exposing Henry to a "'severe shock . . . is, I must confess, a reproach to my management of the case, but,'" he defensively adds, "'we had no means of foreseeing the terrible and paralysing spectacle which the beast presented, nor could we predict the fog which enabled him to burst upon us at short notice'" (166). As Holmes's words suggest, the shockingly unexpected functions as a weapon in the struggle for power: power which Stapleton attempts to wield over Henry and the detectives, and which Holmes attempts to exert over not only the criminal but also (in a less aggressive form) his own immediate society. Contrived by Stapleton, the "paralysing spectacle" of the hound momentarily subdues its audience, robbing them of agency and thereby enforcing the criminal's authority. In Watson's description of the effects of the hound's sudden, horrifying appearance, Holmes's eyes

> started forward in a rigid, fixed stare, and his lips parted in amazement. At the same instant Lestrade gave a yell of terror and threw himself face downwards upon the ground. I sprang to my feet, my inert hand grasping my pistol, my mind paralysed by the dreadful shape which had sprung out upon us from the shadows of the fog. . . . So paralysed were we by the apparition that we allowed him to pass before we had recovered our nerve. (150–51)

The scene depicts a struggle for mastery as Stapleton through his drama creates and unnerves an audience, and as the detectives endeavor to free themselves from that passivity and regain their self-control.

The masterful individual who seeks to control others' nerves must also control his own,[4] and here Holmes (though momentarily stunned) quickly regains his composure. Indeed, Holmes recovers so well that at the end of his investigation he is immediately able to set his "memories of the past" aside to focus "his clear and logical mind" (158) on his next case. While the adventure leaves Henry with "shattered nerves" (158) and even the steady Watson with "scenes which are indelibly fixed in every detail upon [his] memory" (100), Holmes seems relatively untouched by the experience, claiming in "A Retrospection" that his most recent case "'has blurred [his] recollection of Baskerville Hall'" (159). Holmes, who yawns at the close of Mortimer's reading of the

Baskerville legend (14), becomes such a figure of control that the reader measures those rare moments when "the man of iron [is] shaken to the soul" (128) as extraordinarily powerful. Like the detective with whom he is matched in this shocking adventure, Stapleton also possesses self-mastery, a quality demonstrated as he stoops over the corpse of Selden in chapter 12. As Holmes observes,

> "What a nerve the fellow has! How he pulled himself together in the face of what must have been a paralysing shock when he found that the wrong man had fallen a victim to his plot. I told you in London, Watson, and I will tell you now again, that we have never had a foeman more worthy of our steel." (134)

Holmes, who in London had praised his antagonist's cunning—his ability to plot and to shock—here admires his "nerve"—his ability to resist "shock" and the "paralysing" submission it enforces.

Of course, Holmes triumphs in the game with Stapleton: ultimately, the criminal proves less cunning, as he becomes entrapped in the detective's counterplot, and less composed, as he nervously flees, like his own victims, to his death. The absence of Stapleton's body necessarily disturbs the tidiness of the detective's case—raising the slightest possibility that the criminal has eluded justice—but "if the earth told a true story" (156) he has been effectively punished by the great Grimpen Mire. What proves more unsettling, however, is the notion that the force of tyranny is not fully contained in Stapleton and thus conveniently imprisoned in the mire at the novel's end. In one sense, the curse of the Baskervilles is the burden of heredity by which not only positive but negative traits are passed on, so that the characteristics of Hugo can re-emerge in descendants like Stapleton. Holmes can eliminate one tainted individual but not the continuing transmission of genetic traits, which complicates and frustrates ostensible patterns of progress by re-introducing the primitive—the "'throw-back'"

(139) Stapleton or Selden whose "animal face," Watson suggests, "might well have belonged to one of those old savages who dwelt in the burrows on the hill-sides" (97).[5] But even if we ignore the curse of heredity and the traces of prehistoric society that haunt and ironically frame the novel's action, the victory over Stapleton and the progress it implies remain problematic. For the investigation does not so much eradicate oppression and create liberty as it reconfirms and thus strengthens Holmes's own powers of control.

While Holmes is obviously useful in identifying and countering the criminal plot, his victory creates an uneasy resolution. The triumph over oppressive authority perhaps seems straightforward, symbolized as it is by the scene in which Holmes and his assistants burst into the locked upstairs room of the Stapleton house and free the "tied . . . swathed and muffled" (153) figure of Mrs. Stapleton. Indeed, this unbinding might unequivocally signal the return of liberty if the crucial actions were not directed by Holmes, whose dominance disturbingly resembles the villain's own assertions of power. Just as Stapleton seeks to control Mrs. Stapleton, Laura Lyons, Charles and Henry Baskerville, and, of course, the hound itself, so Holmes subjects Henry, the dutiful Watson, the "reverential" Lestrade (146), and the "faithful" Cartwright (140) to his authority. In such relationships power defines itself against vulnerability—against mental weakness (as in the hound), physical weakness (as in the women), and nervous and/or emotional weakness (as in most of the characters). Unsavory as it is, Stapleton's exploitation of the affection of his wife and Laura Lyons cannot be entirely dissociated from the way Holmes uses Watson and Cartwright. Holmes's rather callous comments on " 'my faithful Cartwright, who would certainly have pined away at the door of my hut as a dog does at his master's grave if I had not set his mind at rest about my safety' " (140), underline the emotional dependency of the lad of fourteen; here the basic inequality of a relationship between seasoned detective and young agent is perversely widened to express the subservience of dog to master. A similar servility pervades the relationship of Watson to Holmes, where the connection between two adults is refashioned as one between a childish assistant, keenly seeking praise and approval, and his "master" (115). Watson is devoted to Holmes and he remains constant, even when he is reminded of the gulf that separates him from the great detective, and of his own employment as a tool in cracking the case. " 'Then you use me, and yet do not trust me!' " (124) Watson cries when he discovers Holmes as the watchful man on the tor. A wall of privacy keeps Holmes and many of the details of his project hidden as he supervises his agents—Watson, Cartwright and, particularly at the close, Henry—who blindly follow his directions. As Stapleton also recognizes, there is power in such privacy: power, of course, in the very trick of remaining unseen and unknown as one's plot is deployed, but also power in maintaining an emotional hiddenness, a controlling distance between oneself and the human tools of one's trade.

The unbinding of Mrs. Stapleton, then, may not be without irony. As soon as this " 'dupe and . . . tool' " (154) of Mr. Stapleton is freed, she is recruited by Holmes, who directs her behavior: " 'You bear him no good will, madam. . . . Tell us, then, where we shall find him. If you have ever aided him in evil, help us now and so atone' " (154). Laura Lyons also becomes useful to Holmes, who frees her from Stapleton's influence in order to subject her to his own. By strategically informing Lyons of Stapleton's marriage, Holmes guides her to a recognition that she " 'was never anything but a tool in [Stapleton's] hands' " (144) and thus to a desire to assist the detective. In his control, Holmes becomes disturbingly like his criminal counterpart, whose egoistic passion for collecting ranges from moths and butterflies to a wife who is bound in place beside them in his "museum" (153). Holmes's management of his environment is indicated not only by the results, represented by "the Baker Street collection" (140) and his "indexed list of cases" (158), but also by his investigatory procedure, which involves administering people and assigning them their functions. This work culminates in the series of "orders" given in chapter 13 as Holmes prepares for restaging the "tragedy," but, as he tells Watson, he has been superintending the action from the start: "'When I was watching Stapleton, Cartwright was frequently watching you, so that I was able to keep my hand upon all the strings'" (165). In Watson's assessment, Holmes is "masterful" (146), and significantly the same adjective describes a dangerous propensity in the Baskervilles, "that long line of high-blooded, fiery, and masterful men" (54). For it is in Hugo's kidnapping of the maiden and Stapleton's murderous plotting that we clearly recognize the violence inherent in mastery, a violence that in these instances threatens not only others but also, ironically, the very survival of the Baskerville family itself.

In a sense Stapleton's war against his family represents the bringing under siege of the Baskerville familial body by its own flawed genetic material. But, in opposition to this threat, the novel suggests the possibility of a more optimistic plot-line connected to the restoration of the Baskerville estate. As Mortimer remarks,

> "In these days of *nouveaux riches* it is refreshing to find a case where the scion of an old county family which has fallen upon evil days is able to make his own fortune and to bring it back with him to restore the fallen grandeur of his line. Sir Charles, as is well known, made large sums of money in South African speculation. More wise than those who go on until the wheel turns against them, he realized his gains and returned to England with them. It is only two years since he took up his residence at Baskerville Hall, and it is common talk how large were those schemes of reconstruction and improvement which have been interrupted by his death. Being himself childless, it was his openly expressed desire that the whole countryside should, within his own lifetime, profit by his good fortune, and many will have personal reasons for bewailing his untimely end." (15)

The description of "the fallen grandeur of his line," like the later reference to "that long line of high-blooded, fiery, and masterful men" (54), suggests how recent generations of the family form a "line" or narrative pattern of failure. The first phrase indicates the regressive direction of the family's fortunes, while the second implies the connection between inherited characteristics and a process of repetition that confines the family to its fallen state. Yet Charles, as a figure of change, as one adaptable to a capitalist world, had seemed capable of breaking the pattern of sameness and of creating a plot that would (at least in a financial sense) typify progress. For the *Devon County Chronicle* (although perhaps not for a reader critical of "South African speculation") Charles provides a "refreshing" example of a member of "an old county family" who competes in the new economic order and "make[s] his own fortune." Unlike Stapleton, who controls his nerves but not his egoistic desires, Charles restrains the greed, the "foul passions" (11) that have afflicted the family and condemned it to the downturn of the "wheel" of fortune. Such self-discipline is reflected not only in the prudent behavior of realizing "his gains" before "the wheel turns against" him, but also in the regulation of self (of the characteristic familial selfishness) that prompts his "desire that the whole countryside should . . . profit by his good fortune." While Charles's schemes are "interrupted by his death," Henry renews the effort "to restore the grandeur of his family" (84), thus raising the suspenseful question of whether or not the narrative will unfold as a plot of *progress*. That would seem to depend on Holmes's success; for, as if by a clumsy sleight of hand, the thorny problem of the Baskerville blood-line and character is translated into a puzzle to be solved by a skillful practitioner from outside the family circle. In other words, the troubling notion of the "sins of the fathers"—of inherited sin and its counterpart, inherited genetic deficiency—is reworked within the reassuring structure of detective fiction so that general guilt becomes no more than an overhanging taint of suspicion that instantly evaporates upon solution, when specific guilt is assigned and general innocence affirmed.

While the detective's solution might superficially reassure, the novel seems to subvert such closure by revealing how unsatisfactorily Holmes responds to the deepest anxieties of the text. Like the skeptical titles of Mortimer's essays—"Is Disease a Reversion?," "Some Freaks of Atavism," "Do We Progress?" (6)—the novel plays with the tension between progress and reversion. Although investigation might seem to free Henry Baskerville from the oppressive past, its very method of recovering and, in this case, restaging the criminal act illuminates how the past continues to intrude upon the present. Traits reappear just as shocks recur and the masterful Holmes assumes the authority held by Stapleton. Thus *The Hound of the Baskervilles* is perhaps not so much about change as it is about lack of change. Indeed, in an odd way the novel depicts not so much the desire to wrestle free as the willing acceptance of that sameness, the discovery in the continuing dynamic of authority and submission of a thrill of pleasure.

That submissiveness can generate pleasure as well as pain is effectively illustrated by Watson's ambivalent commentary on Holmes's mastery. As we have seen, Watson seems to censure Holmes's desire to "dominate and surprise" and to create "trying" circumstances under which his assistant "often suffered" (146). But Watson's criticism deconstructs itself; not only does he wonder at the beginning "if, indeed, one may call it a defect," but he also suggests the agreeable excitement of such suspense in his description of how his "nerves thrilled with anticipation" (146). What Watson describes is analogous to the reader's pleasurable submission to the nervous trials of the text—a connection the doctor recognizes as he translates the adventure into a reading experience. In commenting how in "this singular narrative . . . I have tried to make the reader share those dark fears and vague surmises which clouded our lives so long, and ended in so tragic a manner" (155), Watson voices an understanding of the enjoyments of suffering, even as he recreates another version of the exchange between authority and submission. The reader will want to undergo the anguish of suspense even though doing so will mean being victimized by the forceful Watson, who has attempted to "make" us "share those dark fears and vague surmises."

In this figurative relationship the reader assumes a masochistic position, while Watson functions as a sado-masochist. He recreates suffering as a narrative experience, thus establishing a readerly situation with which he fully empathizes. Indeed, as Kaja Silverman contends, it is this identification with the other that distinguishes sado-masochism from sadism:

> the inflicting of pain is indeed incidental to the sado-masochist's pleasure, since that pleasure turns upon an externalizing identification with the masochist. . . . Sadism proper, on the other hand, concerns itself not at all with the object of its cruelty . . . its goal is the sadist's self-engrossing repudiation of otherness.[6]

Whereas Holmes's method of surprising and dominating others may seem implicitly sadistic—an expression of superiority and power—Watson's techniques of suspense are conceived as an attempt to "share" his experience and thereby create a bond with his readers. Thus Watson, who feels the shocks and trials of anticipation that Holmes creates, carefully duplicates those effects for our satisfaction, so that potentially we too are jolted by the sudden appearance of the detective at the end of chapter 11, and we too journey suspensefully into the dark unknown in chapter 14. But Watson, of course, is subject to thrills, such as Selden's death, that are not of Holmes's making, and he is equally adept in conveying those moments. And when Watson reports to a specific reader in Holmes himself, he similarly seeks to engage his audience, intentionally concluding his first report "upon my top note with Barrymore at the window, and now" beginning his second with the promise of information "which will, unless I am much mistaken, considerably surprise you" (82).[7] For the reserved Holmes is, after all, the reader Watson most wishes to unnerve and thus victimize, to draw down into that position of vulnerability with which he himself so closely identifies.

If Watson empathizes with the reader, we in turn identify with Watson as we bear our anxieties of suspense. Theoretically, we could easily escape our plight by either forgoing the novel or turning immediately to its resolution, but we endure the prolonged period of "those dark fears and vague surmises" because we, in fact, enjoy it.[8] From this masochistic perspective, the compulsion to read detective fiction, to return repeatedly to the scene of the crime, perhaps involves not so much an identification with the problem-solving detective as an empathy with the suffering of the fiction's victims. This empathy seems particularly strong in *The Hound of the Baskervilles,* where the nature of the crime—the infliction of sudden shock and fear—facilitates the readers' identification with not only Watson but also Henry, Selden, Charles, Hugo, and the maiden. Through this chain of identification we attempt to make our way back to the supremely horrifying moment that shakes its victims free from their moorings in the here and now. The witlessness and death that the terrifying shock produces come to represent a transcendence of mind and body, a notion, however deluded, of being part of a larger life force. It is for that legendary moment of unbearable sensation, of ecstatic liberation when the fallen victim is sacrificed to, and subsumed by, the supernatural or divine presence of the hound, that the reader vicariously searches.

The masochistic reader, then, seeks the very moment that the novel's ostensible rationalism dismisses as fictive. Indeed, in opposition to the principal thread of detective fiction in which the reader identifies with the investigator's task of constructing order and gaining power, the novel develops a counter form of reading that privileges disorder and disempowerment. By constantly repeating the scene of suffering and thus creating a series of victims extending from the kidnapped maiden to the supposedly fearful reader of Watson's narrative, the novel illustrates its own avoidance of closure: the original dynamic of authority and submission, though muted, remains. If, at first glance, Holmes and Watson appear to have entirely succeeded it is because they have reshaped the opposition of power and vulnerability into configurations that at least seem unproblematic. Instead of objecting to Watson's forceful narrative designs, his readers find pleasure in their submission to the text. Similarly, Watson embraces his friendship with Holmes, even though that relationship subjects him to both nervous shocks and emotional trauma. In recording his constant and anxious search for Holmes's approval, Watson publicly abases himself, so that his own independence disappears and he becomes truly an agent or adjunct of the detective.[9] This renouncing of himself before the great Holmes, who provides him with a sense of value and meaning, suggestively becomes the psychological equivalent of the physical sacrifice of Hugo to the hound. Yet just as readers willingly submit to the narrative that unnerves them, and just as Watson fashions his own subservience to Holmes, so the more obvious victims, on reconsideration, seem almost to invite their own dissolution. Although Charles is horrified by the legend of the hound that roams the moor at night, he is "'in the habit every night before going to bed of walking down the famous Yew Alley of Baskerville Hall'" (16); furthermore, when confronted with the menace, he actually "'run[s] *from* the house instead of towards it,'" as Holmes points out (28). Likewise, Hugo seems to race towards his own immolation, for he, in fact, "'cried aloud before all the company that he would that very night render his body and soul to the Powers of Evil if he might but overtake the wench'" (12). In the context of this Faustian bargain, chasing her becomes an expression of his own willingness—even desire—to become a victim.

In explaining his case to Watson in "A Retrospection," Holmes muses on the control Stapleton exerted over his wife: " 'There can be no doubt that Stapleton exercised an influence over her which may have been love or may have been fear, or very possibly both, since they are by no means incompatible emotions' " (166). In thus linking "love" and "fear," Holmes suggests the masochistic fascination with victimization, a theory, however, that seems inapplicable to the experience of Mrs. Stapleton, whose suffering is anything but pleasurable. Indeed, considering her plight returns us to an unambiguous world in which the boundary between the controlling oppressor and the unwilling victim is clearly drawn. The "clear red weal of a whiplash across her neck" and the "bruises" on her arms testify to how her brutal husband has imprinted his power on her body; but, as she proclaims, " 'this is nothing—nothing! It is my mind and soul that he has tortured and defiled' " (154). Yet even here the category of victim appears slightly unsettled, for ultimately pain and humiliation, in the very process of erasing who she is, seem to liberate her from her culturally constructed role as the submissive woman. Significantly, when the detectives reach her in her imprisonment, her "figure" is "so swathed and muffled in sheets . . . that one could not for the moment tell whether it was that of a man or a woman" (153). Despite "threats" and "blows" she " 'proved unexpectedly independent' " (161), and eventually " 'turned suddenly against him,' " mounting such a challenge to her husband's authority that, as Holmes concludes, " 'if we had not been there, his doom would none the less have been sealed' " (167). Similarly, intense anguish seems to free the imprisoned maiden, who " 'in the stress of her fear . . . did that which might have daunted the bravest or most active man, for by the aid of the growth of ivy which covered . . . the south wall, she came down from under the eaves, and so homeward across the moor' "

(11–12). Just as Watson, in a sense, loses his gendered self—is unmanned by both shocks and the prospect of Holmes's disapproval—so Mrs. Stapleton and the maiden escape, or perhaps find, themselves in the crisis of their very different suffering.

This discussion of *The Hound of the Baskervilles* began with a consideration of ironic patterns of reversal—of how the hunter becomes the hunted, and the victor the victim. But is not the position of the victim also unstable and reversible? Paradoxically, may there not occasionally be pleasure in pain or perhaps a kind of liberation in the suffering that unnerves, decenters, and even abolishes the self?

Conclusion

An investigation of early detective fiction reveals that the very form that emphasizes the piecing together of narrative pattern also incorporates a contradictory impulse that subverts that story-making process. Even as early works of detection plant the evidence their fictional investigators discover and structure into solutions, they also disperse additional clues to complicate that first reading. Indeed, Caleb Williams's investigation culminates not with his recognition of Falkland's guilt, which occurs relatively early in the novel, but with his eventual recognition of his own culpability as a detective and storyteller. Caleb, however, is unusual in detecting himself; in most cases only the reader attends to those clues that challenge the authority of the fictional detective. For as readers we conduct the most extensive investigation, examining not only the narrative design the detective constructs but also the designs or motives underpinning his inquiries.

And what we find tends to undermine the detective's tidy explanations and thus to restore some mystery and complexity to the fictional world.

Why, we might wonder, does nineteenth-century detective fiction critique the very investigations it unfolds? Certainly, suspicion of fictional detectives reflects a general distrust of the law, but it also suggests a more specific anxiety—namely, the authors' uneasiness about their own authority as storytellers. After all, what do the plots of nineteenth-century detective fiction represent but human scheming—both at the level of the conflict between fictional detectives and criminals, and at the level of the ingenious author who contrives the twists and turns of narrative? An author could, of course, attempt to justify these fictions by arguing that they expose the social crimes inherent in "things as they are," a mission which *Caleb Williams, Bleak House,* and *The Moonstone* seriously fulfill. Or he could, for example, maintain that detective fictions celebrate the power of reason, an argument that seems particularly appropriate to the Dupin and Holmes stories. Nevertheless, the doubt might persist that the story is just a story—not reflecting, for example, providential design and authority or even noble intent so much as the desire for a wide readership and commercial success. The author's skepticism of the detective's motives thus becomes skepticism of his own motives as author, of his own desire to exert power over his readers and to draw them into his fictive worlds. How successfully, an author might wonder, have I borne the responsibilities of authorship?

Most readers of detective fiction, however, regard the ability to construct a compelling story as a laudable skill, and most writers of detective plots seem, at least, to share that view. In such works plot suggests not only an effect (the intricately wrought narrative that readers delightedly follow) but also a cause (the authorial planning or plotting that predates the writing). Godwin, in words that seem to express the calculated efforts of the writers who would follow his foray into detection, describes how he prepared to write *Caleb Williams:* "I formed a conception of a book of fictitious adventure, that should in some way be distinguished by a very powerful interest." To create that "powerful interest," Godwin planned his novel backward, from the third volume to the first: "An entire unity of plot would be the infallible result; and the unity of spirit and interest in a tale truly considered, gives it a powerful hold on the reader, which can scarcely be generated with equal success in any other way."[1] Yet even as writers of detective fiction pursue their strategies of creating "a powerful hold on the reader," they seem uneasy about their intentions. In the evidence of the stories themselves and particularly in the conduct of the fictional detective we find not only a celebration of storytelling craft but also a criticism of narrative power. The controlling author is figured as the controlling detective, an egoistic character like Dupin, Bucket, and Holmes who often delights in displaying his ingenuity and in impressing his storytelling power upon his audience. Indeed, the relationship which the figurative teller forms with his listeners becomes an adversarial one with the authorial detective employing the weapon of shock to enforce a powerful distance between the strength of his foresight and self-possession and the weakness implicit in others' ignorance and nervous surprise.

As well as representing anxieties about power, these texts also seem to register discomfort with the particular pleasures of detective fiction. Although the works are apparently designed to entertain the reader by providing "a powerful interest," they simultaneously portray the procuring of writerly and readerly enjoyment as a transgressive activity. In these stories about the making of stories, the authorial detective often emerges as a solitary figure who achieves his private pleasures at others' expense. Holmes, whose laugh "always boded ill to somebody" (*Hound,* 140), obtains enjoyment by triumphing over his opponents. Similarly, Dupin derives pleasure from his investigative victories, remarking, for example, in "The Murders in the Rue Morgue" that he is "'satisfied with having defeated [the Prefect] in his own castle'" (135). And Caleb depicts his investigation of his employer, Falkland, as a mental quest for "satisfaction" (122). Crime and its attendant suffering provide the opportunity for the pleasure the detective finds in the thrill of the investigation and in the resolution of the victory, when he proves his superiority to the mystery, the criminal, and the rival detectives. Although the detective ostensibly serves the interests of the community, his motives seem particularly egoistic and antisocial; moreover the bachelor status of so many fictional detectives seems intended as a further sign of their opposition to the community and its shared pleasures. Reaching the conclusion that Falkland is a murderer, the bachelor Caleb enjoys the "rapture" of mental masturbation:

> . . . I hastened into the garden, and plunged into the deepest of its thickets. My mind was full almost to bursting. I no sooner conceived myself sufficiently removed from all observation, than my thoughts forced their way spontaneously to my tongue, and I exclaimed in a fit of uncontrolable enthusiasm: "This is the murderer! the Hawkinses were innocent! I am sure of it! I will pledge my life for it! It is out! It is discovered! Guilty upon my soul!" (129)

Caleb's climax, in which he ejaculates his verdict and, in a sense, completes his detective narrative, is both a private and (in the anxiety to preserve that privacy) a guilty pleasure. As we read in the next paragraph, Caleb "gave vent to the tumult of [his] thoughts in involuntary exclamations" (129); his "blood boiled within" him (129); in "the very tempest and hurricane of the passions, [he] seemed to enjoy the most soul-ravishing calm" (130). Caleb's activity, like the sadistic practices of another bachelor, Holmes, is self-centered, an image of detection and, by implication, of authorship and reading as self-indulgent, as (paradoxically) an irresponsible retreat from the persistent demands of the world.

Early detective fiction conveys an ambivalence not only about what happens inside the fictional world (the conduct of the detective and the legitimacy of his investigation) but also, it seems, about what happens outside (the behavior of the author and of the reader of that fiction). The fictional representation of the detective's power and pleasure seems a reflection of the author's own anxieties about both the significance and authority of his own narrative, and the value of the investigative role into which he casts the reader. Does the author's narrative power lure the reader into a pastime that is not only frivolous and (in its provision of private pleasure) indulgent but also morally dangerous? The damaging effects of investigation on the fictional detective are suggested by Betteredge's term "detective-fever." But the deleterious consequences of reading itself are suggested by the career of Caleb Williams, whose addictive consumption of stories as a youth trains him to be a detective—to crave (and to expect to find) solutions and the simplistic fulfillment of narrative patterns in the *real* world. Godwin's novel, of course, counteracts the potentially harmful effects implicit in such reading by undermining its own investigative structure and denying the closure that it initially seeks. Similarly, although not as emphatically, the fictions of Poe, Dickens, Collins, and Doyle seem distrustful of the structure of detection and its manipulation of the reader; they too subvert their own narrative projects, thus making the reader wise to the problems of solution and tolerant of the complexities of mystery.

Just as detective fictions paradoxically make the reader tolerant of mystery, they themselves become more tolerant of the reader's pleasure, and not just because that pleasure inevitably becomes allied with a process of instruction. By the time *The Hound of the Baskervilles* (1902) appears at the beginning of the twentieth century, the implied reader of narrative is not so much a victim of the text's machinations as one who willingly chooses to submit to the text's power. *The Moonstone* (1868) playfully encourages the investigating reader to experience its textual pleasures, but it does so in the context of the temptation and guilt generated by its characters, who constantly struggle against the supposed dangers of detection. In Doyle's novel, however, that residue of guilt and victimization seems to disappear. In exploring the relationship between author and reader as figured in the pairings of Holmes with Watson, and Watson with his putative readers, Doyle's novel seems to develop a greater acceptance of pleasure for pleasure's sake. Holmes enjoys a sadistic power in astonishing Watson, but Watson, like Doyle's reader, knowingly and pleasurably accepts his experience with Holmes. Holmes's power, which initially seems to produce only his own egoistic pleasure, becomes necessary to the satisfaction of Watson, just as the power of the narrating Watson, who recreates the nervous trials of the adventure, becomes essential to our masochistic enjoyment as his figurative readers. Like a reader familiar with both the conventions of the developing genre of detective fiction and the conventions of the series of stories chronicling Holmes's investigations, Watson knows what to expect. Watson is not cast by Holmes in a submissive role; rather Watson, like the reader, intentionally selects that role, a decision that, in a sense, *allows* Holmes to assume the masterful position. At the end of the nineteenth century a reciprocal relationship develops between writer and reader as both share the responsibility for the experience of narrative and its pleasures.

Notes

Introduction

1. Detective fiction, as a number of critics have observed, contains two stories: the concealed story of the crime and the visible story of the investigation, which unfolds as the uncovering (or figurative writing) of the criminal story. See, for example, Dennis Porter, *The Pursuit of Crime: Art and Ideology in Detective Fiction* (New Haven: Yale Univ. Press, 1981), 29.

2. I opt for the convenient "his" because the fictional detectives I discuss are male. The period, however, also introduces female investigators such as Marian Halcombe of Collins's thriller *The Woman in White* (1860) and Valeria Macallan of Collins's *The Law and the Lady* (1875). For a discussion of early women detectives see the opening chapters of Patricia Craig's and Mary Cadogan's *The Lady Investigates: Women Detectives and Spies in Fiction* (London: Victor Gollancz, 1981).

3. See Michel Foucault's description of the discipline enforced by "a generalized surveillance" (209) in *Discipline and Punish: The Birth of the Prison,* trans. Alan Sheridan (New York: Vintage Books, 1979), 195–228.

4. The works that have been most helpful to my own thinking about nineteenth-century detective fiction are Ian Ousby's *Bloodhounds of Heaven: The Detective in English Fiction from Godwin to Doyle* (Cambridge, Mass.: Harvard Univ. Press, 1976); D. A. Miller's *The Novel and the Police* (Berkeley: Univ. of California Press, 1988), and Alexander Welsh's

George Eliot and Blackmail (Cambridge, Mass.: Harvard Univ. Press, 1985). Significant studies of detective and crime fiction include Glenn W. Most and William W. Stowe, eds., *The Poetics of Murder: Detective Fiction and Literary Theory* (New York: Harcourt, 1983); Robin Winks, ed., *Detective Fiction: A Collection of Critical Essays* (Englewood Cliffs, N.J.: Prentice-Hall, 1980); Bernard Benstock and Thomas F. Staley, eds., *British Mystery Writers, 1860–1919. Dictionary of Literary Biography. Vol. 70* (Detroit: Gale Research, 1988); Porter's *The Pursuit of Crime*; Martin A. Kayman, *From Bow Street to Baker Street: Mystery, Detection and Narrative* (London: Macmillan, 1992); Stephen Knight, *Form and Ideology in Crime Fiction* (London: Macmillan, 1980); Julian Symons, *Bloody Murder: From the Detective Story to the Crime Novel* (New York: Penguin, 1985); A. E. Murch, *The Development of the Detective Novel* (London: Peter Owen, 1968); Martin Priestman, *Detective Fiction and Literature: The Figure on the Carpet* (London: Macmillan, 1990); Anthea Trodd, *Domestic Crime in the Victorian Novel* (London: Macmillan, 1989); Beth Kalikoff, *Murder and Moral Decay in Victorian Popular Literature* (Ann Arbor, Mich.: UMI Research Press, 1986); T. J. Binyon, *"Murder Will Out": The Detective in Fiction* (Oxford: Oxford Univ. Press, 1989); David I. Grossvogel, *Mystery and Its Fictions: From Oedipus to Agatha Christie* (Baltimore: Johns Hopkins Univ. Press, 1979); John G. Cawelti, *Adventure, Mystery, and Romance: Formula Stories as Art and Popular Culture* (Chicago: Univ. of Chicago Press, 1976); Umberto Eco and Thomas A. Sebeok, eds., *The Sign of Three: Dupin, Holmes, Pierce* (Bloomington: Indiana Univ. Press, 1983); Audrey Peterson, *Victorian Masters of Mystery: From Wilkie Collins to Conan Doyle* (New York: Frederick Ungar, 1984).

5. John Douglas and Mark Olshaker, *Mindhunter: Inside the FBI's Elite Serial Crime Unit* (New York: Scribner, 1995), 37.

6. Ousby, 18. Also see Symons, 45. Although I apply the word "detective" to an early investigator such as Caleb Williams, the term, as Ousby notes, "did not gain currency until the middle of the nineteenth century" (29).

7. *Caleb Williams*, ed. David McCracken (London: Oxford Univ. Press, 1982), 259. The emphasis that appears in quotations in this study is in each case the author's own.

8. See "Part I. From Roguery to Respectability" (1–75) in Ousby's study for details of this transformation.

9. Anthea Trodd, in *Domestic Crime in the Victorian Novel,* contends that "widespread middle-class fears of police intrusion and surveillance . . . co-exist uneasily with admiration of police ability to control the 'dangerous classes' outside" (7). Ian Ousby observes that the linking of criminal and detective in *Caleb Williams* "open[s] up a mine for later writers" such as Poe and Doyle (42).

10. See, for example, Rosemary Jann, "Sherlock Holmes Codes the Social Body," *ELH* 57 (1990): 685–708; and Ronald R. Thomas, "The Fingerprint of the Foreigner: Colonizing the Criminal Body in 1890s Detective Fiction and Criminal Anthropology," *ELH* 61 (1994): 655–83.

Chapter 1
Telling Stories: Narrative and Power in Caleb Williams

1. James Thompson, "Surveillance in William Godwin's *Caleb Williams,*" in *Gothic Fictions: Prohibition/Transgression,* ed. Kenneth W. Graham (New York: AMS Press, 1989), 189.

2. William Godwin, *Caleb Williams,* ed. David McCracken (London: Oxford Univ. Press, 1982). McCracken includes, as "Appendix II," Godwin's "Preface" to the "Standard Novels" edition of *Fleetwood* (London: Richard Bentley, 1832), which describes the composition of *Caleb Williams.* References to both the novel and to the 1832 "Preface" to *Fleetwood* are to McCracken's edition and are included parenthetically in the text.

For those who have not recently read the novel (which is presented as Caleb's memoirs), I offer the following plot summary. At the age of eighteen, with both his mother and father dead, Caleb Williams is hired as the secretary of Ferdinando Falkland, a country squire of a gloomy and mysterious disposition. According to Mr. Collins, who relates the squire's history to Caleb, the despondent Falkland "was once the gayest of the gay," but because of a blow to his highly valued honor, he has become "the mere shell" of his former self (9). The first third of the novel unfolds as a story of Falkland's past, suggesting how his wounded pride and ensuing melancholy are rooted in his conflict with the bully Barnabas Tyrrel. In the climax to this history Falkland is publicly beaten (and thus humiliated) by Tyrrel, and, a paragraph later, Tyrrel is discovered murdered, an event that leaves the sensitive Falkland facing rumors that he is the assassin. Although Falkland is acquitted of wrongdoing and Mr. Hawkins and his son convicted and executed for the crime, Caleb is not convinced of Falkland's innocence. To satisfy his curiosity, Caleb investigates his employer with the result that (1) he decides Falkland is guilty, a verdict that Falkland confirms in his own private confession to Caleb; and (2) he becomes, because of his knowledge, an enemy whom Falkland persecutes. The rest of the novel focuses on the suffering of Caleb, who is framed as a robber, imprisoned, and, following his escape, hunted down. When Caleb is finally captured by the ruthless Gines and returned to prison, no one appears to prosecute him. Consequently, he is released, but his misery continues. Refusing to accede to Falkland's demands that he renounce his earlier claims and proclaim Falkland's innocence, Caleb is now subjected to further harassment from Gines, whom Falkland employs to spread rumors about Caleb and thus prevent him from resettling into society. The novel concludes when Caleb, unable to abide his suffering any longer, attempts to turn the tables on Falkland by accusing him of murder. But when Caleb meets the corpse-like Falkland before the magistrate, his feelings toward his opponent appear suddenly to change. Although Caleb does not retract his charges, his intended accusation seems to become a confession in which, overwhelmed by a sense of his own baseness, he celebrates Falkland and exposes his own failings. Falkland is so moved by the speech that he embraces Caleb and publicly admits his own misdeeds.

3. Several critics have detected a verbal or literary struggle in *Caleb Williams.* Jacqueline T. Miller, in "The Imperfect Tale: Articulation, Rhetoric, and Self in *Caleb Williams,*" *Criticism* 20 (1978), discusses how Godwin's "theory of language . . . inform[s] the novel" (367) and describes "the competition for verbal domination" (376) between Caleb and Falkland. Leland E. Warren, in "*Caleb Williams* and the 'Fall' into Writing," *Mosaic* 20 (1987), examines "the power struggle that is social

discourse" (63). Most recently, Kristen Leaver, in "Pursuing Conversations: *Caleb Williams* and the Romantic Construction of the Reader," *Studies in Romanticism* 33 (1994), argues that "social conflict is played out [between Caleb and Falkland] as each character attempts to impose a different set of literary conventions on the other" (595). I develop a sustained discussion of the critique of storytelling in *Caleb Williams,* examining how in a novelistic world of constant trials (of prosecution and self-defence) narratives function as structures of dominance and control. In particular, I trace Caleb's involvement with storytelling, with those acts of plotting which, in inciting and perpetuating conflict, emerge as the cause of "things as they are."

4. In his chapter on *Caleb Williams* in *Bloodhounds of Heaven: The Detective in English Fiction from Godwin to Doyle* (Cambridge, Mass.: Harvard Univ. Press, 1976), Ian Ousby writes that Caleb "as an autobiographer . . . is bent on self-vindication, not self-criticism" (25). An excellent discussion of how Caleb shapes his narrative is found in Eric Rothstein's *Systems of Order and Inquiry in Later Eighteenth-Century Fiction* (Berkeley: Univ. of California Press, 1975), 208–42. Rothstein examines how Caleb attempts "to read life with the system of a novel" (217), and how his rendition of events conflicts with "things as they are." Godwin gives "each particular a triple meaning, as part of Caleb's self-exculpation, part of Caleb's unwitting self-revelation, and part of a moral understanding that includes but goes beyond the other two meanings" (218).

5. While stories of adventure may suggest the open-ended experience of the picaresque, Caleb and the novel itself emphasize narrative as a closed structure, as a movement to "solution." Here Caleb understands narrative as a structure designed to give the reader satisfaction (in nervous excitement and the relief of closure), and this sense of conscious artistry, of calculation, is explicit in Godwin's own remarks on planning the novel: "I formed a conception of a book of fictitious adventure, that should in some way be distinguished by a very powerful interest. Pursuing this idea, I invented first the third volume of my tale, then the second, and last of all the first" (336–37). Caleb's interests in the mechanical, the scientific, and the fictitious seem even more coherent when we consider Godwin's reasoned and systematic attempt to construct an "entire

unity of plot" (337). But even as Godwin's retrospective comments and the novel (with its intricacy and density of intrigue) seem to prize narrative invention, the text simultaneously betrays suspicion of the very authority that manipulates and crafts and plots. Indeed, as constructed designs in which incidents and characters are organized for specific ends, narratives become metaphorical prisons, structures expressing the power of the teller and the weakness of those whose stories are "told."

Godwin's methodical approach to construction, as he foresees the interrelationships between the constituent parts of his narrative, anticipates the careful attention to plotting that characterizes the nineteenth-century novel and especially the development of detective fiction. Poe begins his essay "The Philosophy of Composition" (1846) by referring to Dickens's observation that "Godwin wrote his 'Caleb Williams' backwards" (193). Poe then acknowledges that "every plot, worth the name, must be elaborated to its *dénouement* before anything be attempted with the pen" (193), before going on to outline his procedure in composing "The Raven," a "work [which] proceeded, step by step, to its completion with the precision and rigid consequence of a mathematical problem" (195). See *The Complete Works of Edgar Allan Poe,* ed. James A. Harrison, 17 vols. (New York: AMS Press, 1965), 14: 193–208.

6. Rudolf F. Storch, in "Metaphors of Private Guilt and Social Rebellion in Godwin's *Caleb Williams,*" *ELH* 34 (1967), remarks that curiosity becomes "an instrument of power, of dominion over another soul" (196). On the relationship of knowledge and power, see also Rothstein, 225; Gary Handwerk, "Of Caleb's Guilt and Godwin's Truth: Ideology and Ethics in *Caleb Williams,*" *ELH* 60 (1993): 953–54; and Ousby, 29–35, who offers a fine treatment of Caleb as a spy.

7. The novel's suggestive depiction of Caleb's curiosity and his ecstatic attainment of *knowledge* in the garden has generated considerable discussion. See, for example, Storch, 196; Alex Gold, Jr., "It's Only Love: The Politics of Passion in Godwin's *Caleb Williams*," *Texas Studies in Literature and Language* 19 (1977): 136; B. J. Tysdahl, *William Godwin as Novelist* (London: Athlone Press, 1981), 52–57; Michael DePorte, "The Consolations of Fiction: Mystery in *Caleb Williams*," *Papers on Language and Liter-*

ature 20 (1984): 162; and Kenneth W. Graham, "Narrative and Ideology in Godwin's *Caleb Williams,*" *Eighteenth-Century Fiction* 2 (1990): 227.

8. Storch also uses the phrase "trial within a trial," noting that Caleb "observes Falkland sitting as a magistrate over a case of murder, just as Hamlet watches Claudius watching the mime" (194).

9. As many readers of the novel have discerned, Caleb's progress is linked to an increasing impartiality of vision and a developing awareness of moral complexity in both Falkland and himself. Rothstein discusses Caleb's "deepened realization of character" (234–35). Ousby describes Caleb's discovery "that good and evil, though apparently worlds apart, are in practice bedfellows," and he explains how "the detective and the criminal become inextricably connected" (40). Mitzi Myers, in "Godwin's Changing Conception of *Caleb Williams,*" *SEL* 12 (1972), remarks that "Caleb's psychological and moral progress from innocence to guilt, from self-deceiving selfishness to enlightened impartiality, is the correlative of Falkland's" (602). Also see, for example, Rexford Stamper, "*Caleb Williams*: The Bondage of Truth," *The Southern Quarterly* 12 (1973): 42–50; C. R. Kropf, "*Caleb Williams* and the Attack on Romance," *Studies in the Novel* 8 (1976): 85–86; Storch, 199; Leaver, 591, 594; and Warren, 65.

10. See Rothstein, who explores the symbolic justness of the hearing in which Caleb is accused of theft and is found to have Falkland's property secreted in his own trunk (225).

11. In his edition of *Caleb Williams,* David McCracken notes that Godwin "used . . . very few quotation marks, preferring instead to let dashes, explanatory comments, or the context indicate a quotation" (xxvi).

12. Stamper has recognized how the rigid categories of innocence and guilt in *Caleb Williams* constrain behaviour: "One must be completely innocent or completely guilty in the eyes of the law" (42).

13. See Thompson for a discussion of surveillance in the novel. Thompson observes that the "horror of surveillance runs throughout *Caleb Williams*" (180) and that "Great Britain becomes one huge Panopticon" (182). Also see the comments of Rothstein on poetic justice: "Caleb has longed to climb into Falkland's skin, and now he must repeat

Falkland's experience" (233). Ousby discusses the reversal by comparing Caleb to the revenger of Jacobean drama whose "fate as victim of his own machinations represents a judgment on his actions" (24).

14. Michel Foucault, in *Discipline and Punish: The Birth of the Prison,* trans. Alan Sheridan (New York: Vintage Books, 1979), writes: "He who is subjected to a field of visibility, and who knows it, assumes responsibility for the constraints of power; he makes them play spontaneously upon himself; he inscribes in himself the power relation in which he simultaneously plays both roles; he becomes the principle of his own subjection" (202–3).

15. On the idea of positive change in the future, see Tilottama Rajan, "Wollstonecraft and Godwin: Reading the Secrets of the Political Novel," *Studies in Romanticism* 27 (1988): 242–43; Graham, 223; McCracken's "Introduction," xv–xvi; and Leaver, 604–5.

16. Rajan, 244.

17. I am drawing a connection between the "representational" nature of both literary characters (like Caleb) and real people. See Michael J. Toolan's comparison of "the semiotic constructedness of people, things, and non-fictional texts" and "the semiotic constructedness of novels" in *Narrative: A Critical Linguistic Introduction* (London: Routledge, 1988), 93.

Chapter 2
The Stories of Poe's Dupin

1. Edgar Allan Poe, *Selected Tales,* ed. Julian Symons (Oxford: Oxford Univ. Press, 1980). All references to the Dupin stories are from this edition and are included parenthetically in the text.

2. J. Gerald Kennedy also discusses how Dupin stuns his opponents in *Poe, Death, and the Life of Writing* (New Haven: Yale Univ. Press, 1987), 120, 124–26.

3. See Julian Symons's comments on the scapegoat in *Bloody Murder: From the Detective Story to the Crime Novel* (New York: Penguin, 1985), 19–20.

4. Shawn Rosenheim points out that "the description of the orang-utan virtually reverses Cuvier's actual claims." See Rosenheim's "Detective Fiction, Psychoanalysis, and the Analytic Sublime," in *The American Face of Edgar Allan Poe,* ed. Shawn Rosenheim and Stephen Rachman (Baltimore: Johns Hopkins Univ. Press, 1995), 161. Also see Burton R. Pollin, "Poe's 'Murders in the Rue Morgue': The Ingenious Web Unravelled," in *Studies in the American Renaissance: 1977,* ed. Joel Myerson (Boston: Twayne, 1978), 253.

5. And in the third story, "The Purloined Letter," Dupin knows the criminal, Minister D—.

6. John Douglas and Mark Olshaker, *Mindhunter: Inside the FBI's Elite Serial Crime Unit* (New York: Scribner, 1995), 32.

7. For a discussion of the figure of Marie, see Laura Saltz's "'(Horrible to Relate!)': Recovering the Body of Marie Rogêt," in *The American Face of Edgar Allan Poe,* ed. Shawn Rosenheim and Stephen Rachman (Baltimore: Johns Hopkins Univ. Press, 1995), 237–67.

8. *The Letters of Edgar Allan Poe,* ed. John Ward Ostrom, 2 vols. (Cambridge, Mass.: Harvard Univ. Press, 1948), 1:200. While I quote from Poe's letter to George Roberts, similar phrasing occurs in his letter of the same day to Joseph Evans Snodgrass (201–2).

9. Quoted in John Walsh's valuable *Poe the Detective: The Curious Circumstances behind "The Mystery of Marie Roget"* (New Brunswick, N.J.: Rutgers Univ. Press, 1968), 55.

10. Ibid., 61.

11. Ibid., 63, 69.

12. The connection of power and narratorial ability is brilliantly treated in Ross Chamber's "Narratorial Authority and 'The Purloined Letter,'" in *The Purloined Poe: Lacan, Derrida and Psychoanalytic Reading,* ed. John P. Muller and William J. Richardson (Baltimore: Johns Hopkins Univ. Press, 1988), which contrasts "the Prefect's failed narrative about his failure [and] Dupin's successful narrative about his success" (292).

13. Many readers of the story have noted similarities between Dupin and the Minister. Joseph J. Moldenhauer, in "Murder as a Fine Art: Basic Connections Between Poe's Aesthetics, Psychology, and Moral Vision," *PMLA* 83 (1968), describes Dupin as "the double of the criminal" and

notes that "the investigator's motives are hardly more philanthropic than the Minister's" (294). Liahna Klenman Babener's "The Shadow's Shadow: The Motif of the Double in Edgar Allan Poe's 'The Purloined Letter,'" in *The Purloined Poe: Lacan, Derrida and Psychoanalytic Reading,* ed. John P. Muller and William J. Richardson (Baltimore: Johns Hopkins Univ. Press, 1988), explores the links between detective and criminal and notes, like my discussion, Dupin's "morally dubious" motives (329–31). Also see, for example, Stephen Knight, *Form and Ideology in Crime Fiction* (London: Macmillan, 1980), 64 and Martin Priestman, *Detective Fiction and Literature: The Figure on the Carpet* (London: Macmillan, 1990), 54.

14. Babener makes a similar point in commenting on how "Dupin likewise employs deception to confound his opponent" (328).

15. Homer's *Odyssey,* 9.473–505.

Chapter 3
"The Narrow Track of Blood": Detection and Storytelling in Bleak House

1. Charles Dickens, *Bleak House,* ed. George Ford and Sylvère Monod (New York: W. W. Norton, 1977). Subsequent references are included parenthetically in the text.

2. Arthur Conan Doyle, *A Study in Scarlet,* in *The Complete Sherlock Holmes* (New York: Doubleday, 1964), 36.

3. Wilkie Collins, *The Woman in White,* ed. Harvey Peter Sucksmith (Oxford: Oxford Univ. Press, 1973), 578.

4. According to J. Hillis Miller in his "Introduction" to *Bleak House* (New York: Penguin, 1971), "the interpretation of signs or of texts may be said to be the fundamental theme of the novel" (17). In "G. M. Reynolds, Dickens, and the Mysteries of London," *Nineteenth-Century Fiction* 32 (1977), Richard C. Maxwell, Jr., writes: "Secrets are suppressed, glossed over and chased after by a myriad of characters" (198). Also see Alexander Welsh, "Blackmail Studies in *Martin Chuzzlewit* and *Bleak House,*" in *Dickens Studies Annual: Essays on Victorian Fiction, Vol. 11,*

ed. Michael Timko, Fred Kaplan, and Edward Guiliano (New York: AMS Press, 1983), 25–35.

5. See Exodus 34:7, and the use of the phrase on pages 211 and 454 of *Bleak House*.

6. See J. Hillis Miller, *Charles Dickens: The World of His Novels* (Cambridge, Mass.: Harvard Univ. Press, 1958), 197; and Mark Spilka, *Dickens and Kafka: A Mutual Interpretation* (Bloomington: Indiana Univ. Press, 1963), 205. For a consideration of guilt and expiation, see Thomas M. Linehan, "Parallel Lives: The Past and Self-Retribution in *Bleak House*," *Studies in the Novel* 20 (1988): 131–50.

7. Christopher Herbert also notes a connection between guilt and goodness; see "The Occult in *Bleak House*," *Novel: A Forum on Fiction* 17 (1984): 109.

8. For an excellent discussion of the traumatic effects of the godmother's speech and Esther's efforts to recover from them, see Alex Zwerdling's "Esther Summerson Rehabilitated," *PMLA* 88 (1973): 429–39.

9. According to J. Hillis Miller in his "Introduction" to *Bleak House*, the novel "locates with profound insight the causes of [society's] sickness in the sign-making power, in the ineradicable human tendency to take the sign for the substance, and in the instinctive habit of interpretation, assimilating others into a private or collective system of meaning" (33–34). Also see Tony Bennett's comments on detective fiction, surveillance, and the "bureaucratic reduction of individuality to a set of knowable traces" in *Popular Fiction: Technology, Ideology, Production, Reading*, ed. Bennett (London: Routledge, 1990), 215.

10. See D. A. Miller's *The Novel and the Police* (Berkeley: Univ. of California Press, 1988), which describes the effectiveness of "law enforcement" (78) in *Bleak House*. While "police power is contained in Bucket, Bucket himself is *not* contained in the way that characters ordinarily are" (79). Also see Michel Foucault's *Discipline and Punish: The Birth of the Prison*, trans. Alan Sheridan (New York: Vintage Books, 1979). Particularly relevant is his discussion of surveillance in the chapter entitled "Panopticism" (195–228).

11. See D. A. Miller, who considers how the presence of public forces of governance, such as the law, encourages the development of private forms of discipline in, for example, the family. "Liberal society and the family were kept free from the carceral institutions that were set up to remedy their failures only by assuming the burden of an immense internal regulation" (59–60).

12. Ian Ousby, in *Bloodhounds of Heaven: The Detective in English Fiction from Godwin to Doyle* (Cambridge, Mass.: Harvard Univ. Press, 1976), discusses how Bucket's detection "near the end of the book . . . becomes useful" (101).

13. J. Hillis Miller makes a similar point in *Charles Dickens: The World of His Novels* (176).

14. Ian Ousby also discusses Bucket's conversational strategies, remarking that the detective "customarily creates whatever image of the other person is most likely to make them subservient to his own ends" (100).

15. Even the taciturn Tulkinghorn demonstrates some storytelling skill in narrating his allegorical tale of "a great lady" whose scandalous past is exposed (505–6).

16. Walter Benjamin, "The Storyteller: Reflections on the Works of Nikolai Leskov," in his *Illuminations,* ed. Hannah Arendt, trans. Harry Zohn (New York: Harcourt, Brace and World, 1968), 101.

Chapter 4
The Detection of Innocence in The Moonstone

1. William Wilkie Collins, *The Moonstone,* ed. Anthea Trodd (Oxford: Oxford Univ. Press, 1982). References are included parenthetically in the text.

2. Peter Thoms, *The Windings of the Labyrinth: Quest and Structure in the Major Novels of Wilkie Collins* (Athens: Ohio Univ. Press, 1992), 140–43.

3. The devotion of the family (particularly its female members) to secrecy is explored by Elisabeth Rose Gruner's "Family Secrets and the

Mysteries of *The Moonstone,*" in *Victorian Literature and Culture, Vol. 21*, ed. John Maynard and Adrienne Auslander Munich (New York: AMS Press, 1993), 127–45.

4. D. A. Miller, in *The Novel and the Police* (Berkeley: Univ. of California Press, 1988), argues that "[n]atural curiosity and common gossip double for an informal system of surveillance observed on the estate long before the Moonstone is stolen" (45); "without having to serve police functions in an ex officio way, gossip and domestic familiarity produce the effect of surveillance; letters and diaries, the effect of dossiers; closed clubs and homes, the effect of punishment" (49).

5. Alexander Welsh, *George Eliot and Blackmail* (Cambridge, Mass.: Harvard Univ. Press, 1985), 81.

6. Welsh has described the "difference that the existence of an effective police force makes in the consciousness of society. On the one hand, just as a reformed criminal law can instill 'potential guilt' in everyone, the presence of police can generate secrets. It behooves a criminal, enmeshed by an efficient network of information, to cover his tracks. It behooves even an innocent person to avoid questioning by keeping his or her affairs as private as possible. As publicity in general enhances the value of privacy, a police force enhances secrecy, or the deliberate enactment of privacy" (91).

7. Cuff develops the "bold experiment" of shocking Rachel with the news of Rosanna's death (190); Blake tries the "experiment" of confronting Rachel at Bruff's home (376), and in his conversation with her "put[s] Mr. Bruff's theory [that Rosanna showed Rachel the stained nightgown] to the test" (381); Jennings conducts "the written experiments" with Candy's "wanderings" that provide "a confirmation of the theory that [he] held" (415); and Mr. Bruff puts his "theory . . . that the Moonstone is in the possession of Mr. Luker's bankers in London" to "the test" (476) by setting a watch upon the bank. Of course, the centerpiece of these efforts is the "experiment" (439) mounted by Jennings "which is to vindicate [Blake's] character in the eyes of other people" (443).

8. Alexander Welsh discusses "the translation of reputation into

information" (82) in *George Eliot and Blackmail,* a book "essentially . . . about the later novels of George Eliot and the culture of information" (v). See particularly "Part II. The Pathology of Information" (30–109).

9. Thoms, 160–61.

10. D. A. Miller describes how "the universality of suspicion gives way to a highly specific guilt. Engaged in producing a social innocence, the detective story might well take for the motto of its enterprise, 'The truth shall make you free'" (34).

11. A number of Collins's earliest reviewers disapproved of the sensational subject matter of fictions such as *Basil* (1852) and *Armadale* (1866), the novel immediately preceding *The Moonstone.* See, for example, the anger of H. F. Chorley (in the *Athenaeum* of 2 June 1866) who, in his review of *Armadale,* wonders "What artist whould choose vermin as his subjects?" Similarly, the reviewer for the *Spectator* (of 9 June 1866) charges Collins in *Armadale* with "overstepping the limits of decency, and revolting every human sentiment." Excerpts of these reviews are found in Norman Page, ed., *Wilkie Collins: The Critical Heritage* (London: Routledge, 1974), 146–48; 149–50.

12. D. A. Miller, in *Narrative and Its Discontents: Problems of Closure in the Traditional Novel* (Princeton: Princeton Univ. Press, 1981), writes, "We might say, generally, that traditional narrative is a quest after that which will end questing; or that it is an interruption of what will be resumed; an expansion of what will be condensed, or a distortion of what will be made straight; a holding in suspense or a putting into question of what will be resolved or answered" (4).

13. For discussions of the sexual suggestiveness of Blake's theft, see Charles Rycroft, "A Detective Story: Psychoanalytic Observations," *Psychoanalytic Quarterly* 26 (1957): 235–38; Sue Lonoff, *Wilkie Collins and His Victorian Readers: A Study in the Rhetoric of Authorship* (New York: AMS Press, 1982), 208–11; and Albert D. Hutter, "Dreams, Transformations, and Literature: The Implications of Detective Fiction," *Victorian Studies* 9 (1975): 200–205.

The anxieties surrounding vision in *The Moonstone* are also noted by Hutter, who links the "excitement and guilt" (206) of observation to the notion of the primal scene in which "the child . . . witnesses parental intercourse" (204). See Hutter, 203–7.

14. In shifting the transgressions of the lovers onto Ablewhite (who is shown to be guilty of both theft and an illicit sexual affair), the detective novelist introduces a twist in the plot that seems as ingenious and as suspicious as any of the strategies of displacement figuratively employed by his characters. On the similarities between Blake and Ablewhite see Hutter, 202–3; Ronald R. Thomas, *Dreams of Authority: Freud and the Fictions of the Unconscious* (Ithaca: Cornell Univ. Press, 1990), 204–5; Alexander Welsh, *Strong Representations: Narrative and Circumstantial Evidence in England* (Baltimore: Johns Hopkins Univ. Press, 1992), 233.

15. For Miller, in *The Novel and the Police,* "the turn in *The Moonstone* from a professional detective to lay detection [practised by the family] acquires its widest resonance as a parable of the modern policing power that comes to rely less on spectacular displays of repressive force than on intangible networks of productive discipline" (51). In Miller's reading, "the family network that detects and judges crime is also empowered to enforce its own sentences," which it does, for example, by shutting its doors to Herncastle (47).

16. Audrey Jaffe comments on "an anxiety about the theatricality of the social world, the susceptibility to manipulation of social identity" (409) in "Detecting the Beggar: Arthur Conan Doyle, Henry Mayhew, and 'The Man with the Twisted Lip.'" See John A. Hodgson, ed., *Sherlock Holmes: The Major Stories with Contemporary Critical Essays* (New York: Bedford Books, 1994), 402–27.

17. Ian Ousby also compares Cuff to Wemmick in *Bloodhounds of Heaven: The Detective in English Fiction from Godwin to Doyle* (Cambridge, Mass.: Harvard Univ. Press, 1976), 121.

18. See, for example, Blake's comments on Cuff's "Metamorphosis" into an "innocent countryman" (486).

Chapter 5
A "Paralysing Spectacle": Authority and Submission in The Hound of the Baskervilles

1. Arthur Conan Doyle, *The Hound of the Baskervilles,* ed. W. W. Robson (Oxford: Oxford Univ. Press, 1994). Page references are included parenthetically in the text.

2. Lawrence Frank detects a different challenge to the detective's case in "Reading the Gravel Page: Lyell, Darwin, and Conan Doyle," *Nineteenth-Century Literature* 44 (1989): 364–87. Frank argues that Doyle in "his Holmes stories . . . offered accounts that seemingly endorsed the historicizing perspective of nineteenth-century science, even as he subtly subverted it by suggesting the fictive nature of the accounts the scientist and the detective offer" (365).

3. Frank (386–87) also comments on this Miltonic echo.

4. See D. A. Miller's chapter, "*Cage aux folles*: Sensation and Gender in *The Woman in White,*" in his *The Novel and the Police* (Berkeley: Univ. of California Press, 1988), 146–91. Particularly relevant are the comments on Count Fosco's "control" (150) and the discussion of "nervousness" and its "association with femininity" (151–56).

5. Christopher Clausen discusses the threat that the "primitive" poses to civilization in "Sherlock Holmes, Order, and the Late-Victorian Mind," in Harold Orel, ed., *Critical Essays on Sir Arthur Conan Doyle* (New York: G. K. Hall, 1992), 82–87. Also see James Kissane and John M. Kissane, "Sherlock Holmes and the Ritual of Reason," *Nineteenth-Century Fiction* 17 (1963): 361–62. In "Sherlock Holmes Codes the Social Body," *ELH* 57 (1990), Rosemary Jann writes that "Holmes advocates the kind of hereditary determinism common in the late nineteenth century, solving 'The Adventure of the Cardboard Box' by detecting a family resemblance in the ears of victim and client, for instance, or realizing that Stapleton must be a Baskerville by his resemblance to the portrait of the evil Sir Hugo. . . . More importantly, moral traits are considered similarly inheritable, so that the abnormal cruelty of a child can incriminate his parents in 'The Copper Beeches' (692). Also see Ronald R. Thomas, "Minding the Body Politic: The Romance of Science and the Revision of

History in Victorian Detective Fiction," *Victorian Literature and Culture* 19 (1991): 247–48.

6. Kaja Silverman, *Male Subjectivity at the Margins* (London: Routledge, 1992), 266. Silverman's discussion of Fassbinder's *In a Year of Thirteen Moons* and particularly her notion of "masochistic ecstasy" (255–70) have been helpful to my consideration of suffering and submission in *The Hound of the Baskervilles.*

7. Watson's attempt to tease Holmes by constructing this suspenseful gap between reports allows Doyle to acknowledge playfully his readers in *The Strand Magazine,* who simultaneously experience a break between the instalments of November and December, 1901.

8. See Silverman's comments on suspense and masochism (198–201).

9. The way in which Watson is absorbed into Holmes is reflected, for example, by the thoughts that burden Watson when he allows Henry to journey out onto the moor alone: "But when I came to think the matter over my conscience reproached me bitterly for having on any pretext allowed him to go out of my sight. I imagined what my feelings would be if I had to return to you and to confess that some misfortune had occurred through my disregard for your instructions. I assure you my cheeks flushed at the very thought. It might not even now be too late to overtake him, so I set off at once in the direction of Merripit House" (85). Although absent, Holmes essentially functions as his agent's "conscience," for the very idea of the detective's disapproval and the feelings it inspires act to regulate Watson's behavior.

Conclusion

1. William Godwin's remarks on the composition of *Caleb Williams* are found in his "Preface" to the "Standard Novels" edition of *Fleetwood* (London: Richard Bentley, 1832). They are also included as "Appendix II" in David McCracken's edition of *Caleb Williams* (London: Oxford Univ. Press, 1982), 335–41.

Works Cited

Babener, Liahna Klenman. "The Shadow's Shadow: The Motif of the Double in Edgar Allan Poe's 'The Purloined Letter.'" In *The Purloined Poe: Lacan, Derrida and Psychoanalytic Reading,* ed. John P. Muller and William J. Richardson, 323–34. Baltimore: Johns Hopkins Univ. Press, 1988.

Benjamin, Walter. *Illuminations.* Ed. Hannah Arendt; trans. Harry Zohn. New York: Harcourt, Brace and World, 1968.

Bennett, Tony, ed. *Popular Fiction: Technology, Ideology, Production, Reading.* London: Routledge, 1990.

Benstock, Bernard, and Thomas F. Staley, eds. *British Mystery Writers, 1860–1919. Dictionary of Literary Biography. Vol. 70.* Detroit: Gale Research, 1988.

Binyon, T. J. *"Murder Will Out": The Detective in Fiction.* Oxford: Oxford Univ. Press, 1989.

Cawelti, John G. *Adventure, Mystery, and Romance: Formula Stories as Art and Popular Culture.* Chicago: Univ. of Chicago Press, 1976.

Chambers, Ross. "Narratorial Authority and 'The Purloined Letter.'" In *The Purloined Poe: Lacan, Derrida and Psychoanalytic Reading,* ed. John P. Muller and William J. Richardson, 285–306. Baltimore: Johns Hopkins Univ. Press, 1988.

Clausen, Christopher. "Sherlock Holmes, Order, and the Late-Victorian Mind." In *Critical Essays on Sir Arthur Conan Doyle,* ed. Harold Orel, 66–91. New York: G. K. Hall, 1992.

Collins, Wilkie. *Armadale.* Ed. Catherine Peters. Oxford: Oxford Univ. Press, 1989.

———. *Basil.* Ed. Dorothy Goldman. Oxford: Oxford Univ. Press, 1990.

———. *The Law and the Lady.* New York: AMS Press, 1970.

———. *The Moonstone.* Ed. Anthea Trodd. Oxford: Oxford Univ. Press, 1982.

———. *The Woman in White.* Ed. Harvey Peter Sucksmith. Oxford: Oxford Univ. Press, 1980.

Craig, Patricia, and Mary Cadogan. *The Lady Investigates: Women Detectives and Spies in Fiction.* London: Victor Gollancz, 1981.

DePorte, Michael. "The Consolations of Fiction: Mystery in *Caleb Williams.*" *Papers on Language and Literature* 20 (1984): 154–64.

Dickens, Charles. *Bleak House.* Ed. George Ford and Sylvère Monod. New York: W. W. Norton, 1977.

Douglas, John, and Mark Olshaker. *Mindhunter: Inside the FBI's Elite Serial Crime Unit.* New York: Scribner, 1995.

Doyle, Arthur Conan. *The Hound of the Baskervilles.* Ed. W. W. Robson. Oxford: Oxford Univ. Press, 1994.

———. *A Study in Scarlet.* In *The Complete Sherlock Holmes,* 13–86. New York: Doubleday, 1964.

Eco, Umberto, and Thomas A. Sebeok, eds. *The Sign of Three: Dupin, Holmes, Pierce.* Bloomington: Indiana Univ. Press, 1983.

Foucault, Michel. *Discipline and Punish: The Birth of the Prison.* Trans. Alan Sheridan. New York: Vintage Books, 1979.

Frank, Lawrence. "Reading the Gravel Page: Lyell, Darwin, and Conan Doyle." *Nineteenth-Century Literature* 44 (1989): 364–87.

Godwin, William. *Caleb Williams.* Ed. David McCracken. London: Oxford Univ. Press, 1982.

Gold, Alex, Jr. "It's Only Love: The Politics of Passion in Godwin's *Caleb Williams.*" *Texas Studies in Literature and Language* 19 (1977): 135–60.

Graham, Kenneth W. "Narrative and Ideology in Godwin's *Caleb Williams.*" *Eighteenth-Century Fiction* 2 (1990): 215–28.

Grossvogel, David I. *Mystery and Its Fictions: From Oedipus to Agatha Christie.* Baltimore: Johns Hopkins Univ. Press, 1979.

Gruner, Elisabeth Rose. "Family Secrets and the Mysteries of *The Moonstone.*" In *Victorian Literature and Culture, Vol. 21,* ed. John Maynard and Adrienne Auslander Munich, 127–45. New York: AMS Press, 1993.

Handwerk, Gary. "Of Caleb's Guilt and Godwin's Truth: Ideology and Ethics in *Caleb Williams.*" *ELH* 60 (1993): 939–60.

Herbert, Christopher. "The Occult in *Bleak House.*" *Novel: A Forum on Fiction* 17 (1984): 101–15.

Hutter, Albert D. "Dreams, Transformations, and Literature: The Implications of Detective Fiction." *Victorian Studies* 9 (1975): 181–209.

Jaffe, Audrey. "Detecting the Beggar: Arthur Conan Doyle, Henry Mayhew, and 'The Man with the Twisted Lip.'" In *Sherlock Holmes: The Major Stories with Contemporary Critical Essays,* ed. John A. Hodgson, 402–27. New York: Bedford Books, 1994.

Jann, Rosemary. "Sherlock Holmes Codes the Social Body." *ELH* 57 (1990): 685–708.

Kalikoff, Beth. *Murder and Moral Decay in Victorian Popular Literature.* Ann Arbor, Mich.: UMI Research Press, 1986.

Kayman, Martin A. *From Bow Street to Baker Street: Mystery, Detection and Narrative.* London: Macmillan, 1992.

Kennedy, J. Gerald. *Poe, Death, and the Life of Writing.* New Haven: Yale Univ. Press, 1987.

Kissane, James, and John M. Kissane. "Sherlock Holmes and the Ritual of Reason." *Nineteenth-Century Fiction* 17 (1963): 353–62.

Knight, Stephen. *Form and Ideology in Crime Fiction.* London: Macmillan, 1980.

Kropf, C. R. "*Caleb Williams* and the Attack on Romance." *Studies in the Novel* 8 (1976): 81–87.

Leaver, Kristen. "Pursuing Conversations: *Caleb Williams* and the Romantic Construction of the Reader." *Studies in Romanticism* 33 (1994): 589–610.

Linehan, Thomas M. "Parallel Lives: The Past and Self-Retribution in *Bleak House.*" *Studies in the Novel* 20 (1988): 131–50.

Lonoff, Sue. *Wilkie Collins and His Victorian Readers: A Study in the Rhetoric of Authorship.* New York: AMS Press, 1982.

Maxwell, Richard C., Jr. "G. M. Reynolds, Dickens, and the Mysteries of London." *Nineteenth-Century Fiction* 32 (1977): 188–213.

Miller, D. A. *Narrative and Its Discontents: Problems of Closure in the Traditional Novel.* Princeton: Princeton Univ. Press, 1981.

———. *The Novel and the Police.* Berkeley: Univ. of California Press, 1988.

Miller, J. Hillis. *Charles Dickens: The World of His Novels.* Cambridge, Mass.: Harvard Univ. Press, 1958.

———. Introduction to *Bleak House,* by Charles Dickens. New York: Penguin, 1971.

Miller, Jacqueline T. "The Imperfect Tale: Articulation, Rhetoric, and Self in *Caleb Williams.*" *Criticism* 20 (1978): 366–82.

Moldenhauer, Joseph J. "Murder as a Fine Art: Basic Connections Between Poe's Aesthetics, Psychology, and Moral Vision." *PMLA* 83 (1968): 284–97.

Most, Glenn W., and William W. Stowe, eds. *The Poetics of Murder: Detective Fiction and Literary Theory.* New York: Harcourt, 1983.

Murch, A. E. *The Development of the Detective Novel.* London: Peter Owen, 1968.

Myers, Mitzi. "Godwin's Changing Conception of *Caleb Williams.*" *SEL* 12 (1972): 591–628.

Ousby, Ian. *Bloodhounds of Heaven: The Detective in English Fiction from Godwin to Doyle.* Cambridge, Mass.: Harvard Univ. Press, 1976.

Page, Norman, ed. *Wilkie Collins: The Critical Heritage.* London: Routledge, 1974.

Peterson, Audrey. *Victorian Masters of Mystery: From Wilkie Collins to Conan Doyle.* New York: Frederick Ungar, 1984.

Poe, Edgar Allan. *The Letters of Edgar Allan Poe.* Ed. John Ward Ostrom. 2 vols. Cambridge, Mass.: Harvard Univ. Press, 1948.

———. "The Philosophy of Composition." In *The Complete Works of Edgar Allan Poe,* ed. James A. Harrison, 14: 193–208. 17 vols. New York: AMS Press, 1965.

———. *Selected Tales.* Ed. Julian Symons. Oxford: Oxford Univ. Press, 1980.

Pollin, Burton R. "Poe's 'Murders in the Rue Morgue': The Ingenious Web Unravelled." In *Studies in the American Renaissance: 1977,* ed. Joel Myerson, 235–59. Boston: Twayne, 1978.

Porter, Dennis. *The Pursuit of Crime: Art and Ideology in Detective Fiction.* New Haven: Yale Univ. Press, 1981.

Priestman, Martin. *Detective Fiction and Literature: The Figure on the Carpet.* London: Macmillan, 1990.

Rajan, Tilottama. "Wollstonecraft and Godwin: Reading the Secrets of the Political Novel." *Studies in Romanticism* 27 (1988): 221–51.

Rosenheim, Shawn. "Detective Fiction, Psychoanalysis, and the Analytic Sublime." In *The American Face of Edgar Allan Poe,* ed. Shawn Rosenheim and Stephen Rachman, 153–76. Baltimore: Johns Hopkins Univ. Press, 1995.

Rothstein, Eric. *Systems of Order and Inquiry in Later Eighteenth-Century Fiction.* Berkeley: Univ. of California Press, 1975.

Rycroft, Charles. "A Detective Story: Psychoanalytic Observations." *Psychoanalytic Quarterly* 26 (1957): 229–45.

Saltz, Laura. "'(Horrible to Relate!)': Recovering the Body of Marie Rogêt." In *The American Face of Edgar Allan Poe,* ed. Shawn Rosenheim and Stephen Rachman, 237–67. Baltimore: Johns Hopkins Univ. Press, 1995.

Silverman, Kaja. *Male Subjectivity at the Margins.* London: Routledge, 1992.

Spilka, Mark. *Dickens and Kafka: A Mutual Interpretation.* Bloomington: Indiana Univ. Press, 1963.

Stamper, Rexford. "*Caleb Williams*: The Bondage of Truth." *The Southern Quarterly* 12 (1973): 39–50.

Storch, Rudolf F. "Metaphors of Private Guilt and Social Rebellion in Godwin's *Caleb Williams.*" *ELH* 34 (1967): 188–207.

Symons, Julian. *Bloody Murder: From the Detective Story to the Crime Novel.* New York: Penguin, 1985.

Thomas, Ronald R. *Dreams of Authority: Freud and the Fictions of the Unconscious.* Ithaca: Cornell Univ. Press, 1990.

———. "The Fingerprint of the Foreigner: Colonizing the Criminal Body in 1890s Detective Fiction and Criminal Anthropology." *ELH* 61 (1994): 655–83.

———. "Minding the Body Politic: The Romance of Science and the Revision of History in Victorian Detective Fiction." *Victorian Literature and Culture* 19 (1991): 233–54.

Thompson, James. "Surveillance in William Godwin's *Caleb Williams.*" In *Gothic Fictions: Prohibition / Transgression,* ed. Kenneth W. Graham, 173–98. New York: AMS Press, 1989.

Thoms, Peter. *The Windings of the Labyrinth: Quest and Structure in the Major Novels of Wilkie Collins.* Athens: Ohio Univ. Press, 1992.

Toolan, Michael J. *Narrative: A Critical Linguistic Introduction.* London: Routledge, 1988.

Trodd, Anthea. *Domestic Crime in the Victorian Novel.* London: Macmillan, 1989.

Tysdahl, B. J. *William Godwin as Novelist.* London: Athlone Press, 1981.

Walsh, John. *Poe the Detective: The Curious Circumstances behind "The Mystery of Marie Roget."* New Brunswick, N.J.: Rutgers Univ. Press, 1968.

Warren, Leland E. "*Caleb Williams* and the 'Fall' into Writing." *Mosaic* 20 (1987): 57–69.

Welsh, Alexander. "Blackmail Studies in *Martin Chuzzlewit* and *Bleak House.*" In *Dickens Studies Annual: Essays on Victorian Fiction, Vol. 11,* ed. Michael Timko, Fred Kaplan, and Edward Guiliano, 25–35. New York: AMS Press, 1983.

———. *George Eliot and Blackmail.* Cambridge, Mass.: Harvard Univ. Press, 1985.

———. *Strong Representations: Narrative and Circumstantial Evidence in England.* Baltimore: Johns Hopkins Univ. Press, 1992.

Winks, Robin, ed. *Detective Fiction: A Collection of Critical Essays.* Englewood Cliffs, N.J.: Prentice-Hall, 1980.

Zwerdling, Alex. "Esther Summerson Rehabilitated." *PMLA* 88 (1973): 429–39.

Index

A Note about the Author

A resident of London, Ontario, Peter Thoms teaches at both King's College and the University of Western Ontario. He is the author of *The Windings of the Labyrinth: Quest and Structure in the Major Novels of Wilkie Collins,* published by Ohio University Press in 1992.